Editor
Eric Migliaccio

Editor in Chief
Ina Massler Levin, M.A.

Creative Director
Karen J. Goldfluss, M.S. Ed.

Illustrator
Renée Mc Elwee

Cover Artist
Brenda DiAntonis

Art Coordinator
Renée Mc Elwee

Imaging
Leonard P. Swierski

Publisher
Mary D. Smith, M.S. Ed.

violin : instrument

crocodile : reptile

A terrific way to:
- Sharpen logical thinking skills
- Prepare for standardized tests
- Understand word relationships
- Improve & develop vocabulary

Teacher Created Resources

TCR 3169

ANALOGIES for Critical Thinking

Author
Ruth Foster, M.Ed.

Teacher Created Resources
12621 Western Avenue
Garden Grove, CA 92841
www.teachercreated.com
ISBN: 978-1-4206-3169-2
©2011 Teacher Created Resources
Reprinted, 2019
Made in U.S.A.

Teacher Created Resources

Table of Contents

Introduction

Think of an analogy as a wonderful puzzle, and one has a great interdisciplinary teaching exercise.

An analogy is a type of comparison. An analogy is when a likeness is found between two unlike things. If approached as a puzzle, one solves the analogy by finding out how the pieces fit together. What links the words to each other? How can they be connected or tied together? What is the relationship between them?

> **cat** is to **meow** as **dog** is to ___**bark**___

Although the example above may appear to be easy, it is an exercise that involves cognitive processes and critical-thinking skills. One must comprehend the words read, categorize them, understand the connection between them, and then find a similar connection between a different pair of words. In this case, both *meow* and *bark* are sounds that a cat and dog make, respectively.

Analogies written for this series will focus on a variety of word relationships. They will develop, reinforce, and expand skills in the following areas:

→ visual imagery

→ reading comprehension

→ paying attention to detail (word sequence within word pairs)

→ vocabulary development

→ synonym, antonym, and homophone recognition and recall

→ understanding different shades of word meanings

→ reasoning

→ standardized-test taking

Students will be able to demonstrate mastery by doing the following:

→ working with both multiple-choice and write-out question formats

→ analyzing and fixing incorrect analogies

→ writing their own analogies in both question and sentence format

For interdisciplinary practice, some analogies will be subject-specific (addressing science, math, or social studies, for example). Others will push students to think outside of the box, as creative and imaginative connections between words will be asked for. Students may then explain in writing or verbally (depending on skill level) how they created analogous word pairs or situations.

Blank answer sheets can be found on page 60. Use these sheets to provide your students with practice in answering questions in a standardized-test format.

Introducing Analogies

Directions: Fill in the word you think should go in the blank.

1. **Dog** is to **puppy** as **cat** is to _____.

2. **Dog** is to **bark** as **duck** is to _____.

3. **Dog** is to **pack** as **cow** is to _____.

4. **Dog** is to **fur** as **bird** is to _____.

5. **Dog** is to **golden retriever** as **bird** is to _____.

What did you just do? You made **analogies!** An analogy is a likeness in some ways between things that are otherwise unlike.

A puppy is not a kitten, but a puppy is like a kitten because they are both kinds of animal babies.

Sometimes analogies are written like this:

> **dog : puppy :: cat : kitten**

- The single colon (:) compares two items in a word pair.
- The double colon (::) compares the first word pair to the second word pair.

6. Rewrite question 2, 3, 4, or 5 in the analogy form using colons.

   _____ : _____ :: _____ : _____

Directions: Fill in the blanks to finish the analogies. There may be more than one correct answer for some. Be prepared to explain each analogy.

7. male : female :: father : _____

8. female : male :: sister : _____

9. male : female :: uncle : _____

10. female : male :: niece : _____

11. father : son :: mother : _____

12. sister : brother :: mother : _____

Synonyms in Analogies

A **synonym** is a word that is nearly the **same** in meaning as another word.

1. Which word is not a synonym of the others?

   (A) ordinary   (B) peculiar   (C) strange   (D) unusual

2. Which answer makes the best analogy?

   (A) ordinary : odd :: peculiar : unusual   (C) strange : peculiar :: odd : ordinary

   (B) unusual : ordinary :: strange : odd   (D) peculiar : odd :: strange : unusual

Directions: Find the synonym that best completes each analogy.

3. **Abundant** is to **teeming** as **limited** is to _____.

   (A) plenty   (B) scarce   (C) lots   (D) sufficient

4. **Elevate** is to **raise** as **drop** is to _____.

   (A) plunge   (B) increase   (C) lift   (D) rain

5. **Cup** is to **glass** as **kettle** is to _____.

   (A) boil   (B) drink   (C) cauldron   (D) plate

6. **Umbrella** is to **parasol** as **scrap** is to _____.

   (A) shade   (B) fragment   (C) protection   (D) whole

7. **Alone** is to **unaccompanied** as **amount** is to _____.

   (A) secluded   (B) quake   (C) quantity   (D) solitary

8. **Explore** is to **discover** as **walk** is to _____.

   (A) search   (B) accelerate   (C) find   (D) ramble

Directions: Write down four answers. Only one answer should be correct!

9. **Energetic** is to **active** as **tired** is to _____.

   (A) _____   (C) _____

   (B) _____   (D) _____

10. Which one of your answers was correct? Write a sentence telling why. Use the word *synonym* in your sentence.

   _____

   _____

Antonyms in Analogies

An **antonym** is a word that is the **opposite** in meaning of another word.

1. Which word is an antonym of the others?

   Ⓐ rejoice   Ⓑ grieve   Ⓒ celebrate   Ⓓ delight

2. Which answer makes the best analogy?

   Ⓐ mourn : rejoice :: delight : celebrate   Ⓒ rejoice : grieve :: celebrate : mourn

   Ⓑ celebrate : delight :: grieve : rejoice   Ⓓ delight : mourn :: rejoice : celebrate

---

Directions: Find the antonym that best completes the analogy.

3. **Question** is to **answer** as **accept** is to _____.

   Ⓐ respond   Ⓑ apply   Ⓒ awaken   Ⓓ reject

4. **Horrible** is to **wonderful** as **vast** is to _____.

   Ⓐ enormous   Ⓑ petite   Ⓒ mammoth   Ⓓ empty

5. **Graceful** is to **clumsy** as **peaceful** is to _____.

   Ⓐ agitated   Ⓑ delicate   Ⓒ calm   Ⓓ tranquil

6. **Float** is to **sink** as **jab** is to _____.

   Ⓐ poke   Ⓑ stab   Ⓒ prod   Ⓓ stroke

7. **Boastful** is to **modest** as **stingy** is to _____.

   Ⓐ generous   Ⓑ miserly   Ⓒ cheap   Ⓓ proud

8. **Expert** is to **amateur** as **identical** is to _____.

   Ⓐ uniform   Ⓑ professional   Ⓒ different   Ⓓ twins

Directions: Write down four answers. Only one answer should be correct!

10. **Patient** is to **impatient** as **healthy** is to _____.

   Ⓐ _____   Ⓒ _____

   Ⓑ _____   Ⓓ _____

11. Which one of your answers was correct? Write a sentence telling why. Use the word *antonym* in your sentence.

_____

_____

Synonym and Antonym Practice

Directions: Choose the answer that best completes the analogy. Write **synonyms** or **antonyms** on the blank line to describe how the question and answer words are related.

- Antonyms are words that are opposite in meaning.

- Synonyms are words that mean the same.

1. **marvelous : great**
- (A) drenched : wet
- (B) silly : serious
- (C) dull : exciting
- (D) gorgeous : ugly

_____

2. **rapid : slow**
- (A) wait : remain
- (B) shrink : increase
- (C) stare : peer
- (D) stop : cease

_____

3. **err : correct**
- (A) teach : educate
- (B) muffle : silence
- (C) aid : hinder
- (D) shout : yell

_____

4. **rival : competitor**
- (A) teacher : student
- (B) doctor : patient
- (C) pilot : airplane
- (D) jester : clown

_____

5. **spry : stiff**
- (A) lucky : fortunate
- (B) tardy : early
- (C) tender : caring
- (D) normal : average

_____

6. **confuse : bewilder**
- (A) squeeze : expand
- (B) employ : hire
- (C) squabble : agree
- (D) mistreat : help

_____

7. **monitor : watch**
- (A) steal : return
- (B) lead : follow
- (C) fracture : break
- (D) plant : uproot

_____

8. **harsh : tender**
- (A) lush : barren
- (B) lazy : sluggish
- (C) happy : cheerful
- (D) lean : slender

_____

9. **flicker : blink**
- (A) insist : demand
- (B) relax : toil
- (C) tighten : loosen
- (D) stumble : leap

_____

10. **legal : lawful**
- (A) shallow : deep
- (B) rigid : supple
- (C) absent : present
- (D) polite : courteous

_____

11. **formal : casual**
- (A) descend : fall
- (B) disappear : vanish
- (C) strict : inexact
- (D) solid : firm

_____

12. **fleeting : momentary**
- (A) ancient : youthful
- (B) tired : weary
- (C) clumsy : graceful
- (D) airy : weighty

_____

Synonym and Antonym Analogies

Directions: Write as many synonyms and antonyms as you can think of for the given words. Then, use a **thesaurus** to add even more words to your list.

	Synonyms	Antonyms
1. sturdy		
2. ridiculous		
3. enchanting		
4. injure		
5. create		

Directions: Write analogy questions using some of the words you wrote down. Two questions should be synonyms. Two questions should be antonyms.

6. _____ : _____
   Ⓐ_____ : _____
   Ⓑ_____ : _____
   Ⓒ_____ : _____
   Ⓓ_____ : _____
   Correct answer: _____ Synonym or antonym: _____

7. _____ : _____
   Ⓐ_____ : _____
   Ⓑ_____ : _____
   Ⓒ_____ : _____
   Ⓓ_____ : _____
   Correct answer: _____ Synonym or antonym: _____

8. _____ : _____
   Ⓐ_____ : _____
   Ⓑ_____ : _____
   Ⓒ_____ : _____
   Ⓓ_____ : _____
   Correct answer: _____ Synonym or antonym: _____

9. _____ : _____
   Ⓐ_____ : _____
   Ⓑ_____ : _____
   Ⓒ_____ : _____
   Ⓓ_____ : _____
   Correct answer: _____ Synonym or antonym: _____

Plurals

Directions: Think about how some words are **singular** (one) or **plural** (more than one). Then choose the answer that best completes each analogy. Pay attention to order!

| tooth : teeth | is not the same as | teeth : tooth |

---

1. tooth : teeth is

- (A) singular : plural
- (B) plural : singular

2. teeth : tooth is

- (A) singular : plural
- (B) plural : singular

---

3. leaf : leaves

- (A) loaves : loaf
- (B) loafes : loaf
- (C) half : halves
- (D) half : halfes

4. mice : mouse

- (A) pie : pies
- (B) dice : die
- (C) sigh : sighs
- (D) tie : ties

5. woman : women

- (A) ox : oxen
- (B) feet : foot
- (C) ladies : lady
- (D) children : child

---

6. people : person

- (A) fungus : fungi
- (B) nucleus : nuclei
- (C) radius : radii
- (D) cacti : cactus

7. piano : pianos

- (A) torpedoes : torpedo
- (B) tomatoes : tomato
- (C) volcanoes : volcano
- (D) potato : potatoes

8. copies : copy

- (A) tries : try
- (B) pass : passes
- (C) baby : babies
- (D) kiss : kisses

---

9. wharf : wharves

- (A) dwarves : dwarf
- (B) life : lives
- (C) wolves : wolf
- (D) thieves : thief

10. cattle : cow

- (A) deer : buck
- (B) fish : school
- (C) men : man
- (D) sun : stars

11. goose : geese

- (A) shirts : shirt
- (B) socks : sock
- (C) jackets : jacket
- (D) pants : pants

---

12. Write your own analogy using singular and plural words. Make sure only one of your answers is correct!

_____ : _____

- (A) _____ : _____
- (C) _____ : _____
- (B) _____ : _____
- (D) _____ : _____

Adjectives

Adjectives are often used in analogies. An adjective is a word that describes a noun. Adjectives answer three questions:

1. What kind is it?   *2.* How many are there?   *3.* Which one is it?

Directions: Fill in the blanks and find the answer that best completes each analogy.

1. In the word pair | **feather : pillow** |, the word __f_____ is an
_____a_____ because it tells what kind of pillow it is.

2. In the word pair | **feather : down** |, the word _____ is an
_____ because it tells what kind of feather it is.

---

3. **can : aluminum**
- Ⓐ plastic : bottle
- Ⓑ leather : ball
- Ⓒ wool : jacket
- Ⓓ hose : rubber

4. **rainy : tropics**
- Ⓐ mountainous : plain
- Ⓑ arid : desert
- Ⓒ lake : salt
- Ⓓ volcano : dormant

5. **pumpkin : orange**
- Ⓐ watermelon : seed
- Ⓑ yellow : maize
- Ⓒ hot : pepper
- Ⓓ spinach : green

6. **moment : brief**
- Ⓐ movie : watch
- Ⓑ eon : long
- Ⓒ year : century
- Ⓓ ruler : measure

7. **wrestler : flexible**
- Ⓐ swimmer : pool
- Ⓑ baseball : catch
- Ⓒ gymnast : limber
- Ⓓ speedy : skater

8. **zebra : striped**
- Ⓐ parrot : colorful
- Ⓑ giraffe : neck
- Ⓒ lion : mane
- Ⓓ hyena : laugh

9. **sharp : scalpel**
- Ⓐ scissors : cut
- Ⓑ peel : orange
- Ⓒ sew : needle
- Ⓓ tart : lemon

10. **dinosaur : ancient**
- Ⓐ tree : acorn
- Ⓑ puppy : wag
- Ⓒ Saturn : distant
- Ⓓ frozen : ice

11. **ocean : vast**
- Ⓐ frog : jumping
- Ⓑ frog : jumps
- Ⓒ frog : jumped
- Ⓓ frog : jump

---

12. Think of three adjectives that might be used to describe each noun.

- snake   _____   _____   _____

- elephant   _____   _____   _____

13. Make an analogy using words and answers from question 12.

_____ : _____ :: _____ : _____

What People Use

Some word pairs in analogies are connected by what people use or need in their jobs.

Examples: baker : oven (*person* to *what he/she uses*)

oven : baker (*what he/she uses* to *person*)

Directions: Choose the answer that best completes each analogy. Then write down other items the person in the question might use.

1. **easel : painter**
   - Ⓐ chisel : sculptor
   - Ⓑ sculptor : chisel
   - Ⓒ pencil : sketch
   - Ⓓ sketch : pencil

   brush,_____

2. **navigator : map**
   - Ⓐ astronaut : space
   - Ⓑ hoe : gardener
   - Ⓒ farmer : tractor
   - Ⓓ pilot : flies

   _____

3. **goggles : swimmer**
   - Ⓐ paddle : canoe
   - Ⓑ helmet : biker
   - Ⓒ pen : paper
   - Ⓓ firefighter : truck

   _____

4. **knight : sword**
   - Ⓐ bow : archer
   - Ⓑ saddle : horse
   - Ⓒ castle : moat
   - Ⓓ climber : rope

   _____

5. **carpenter : hammer**
   - Ⓐ plumber : wrench
   - Ⓑ crane : builder
   - Ⓒ axe : logger
   - Ⓓ computer : writer

   _____

6. **apron : cook**
   - Ⓐ dog : leash
   - Ⓑ shoes : socks
   - Ⓒ scrubs : surgeon
   - Ⓓ stove : boil

   _____

7. **desk : student**
   - Ⓐ teacher : board
   - Ⓑ line : hook
   - Ⓒ captain : ship
   - Ⓓ mitt : catcher

   _____

8. **detective : clue**
   - Ⓐ dalmation : spotted
   - Ⓑ bloodhound : scent
   - Ⓒ retriever : golden
   - Ⓓ Chihuahua : small

   _____

9. **scissors : tailor**
   - Ⓐ horse : jockey
   - Ⓑ needle : sew
   - Ⓒ artist : brush
   - Ⓓ loom : weaver

   _____

10. Write three analogies using some of the items you wrote down.

_____ : _____ :: _____ : _____

_____ : _____ :: _____ : _____

_____ : _____ :: _____ : _____

Things that Go Together

Directions: Write down what you think of when you read these words:

(There are no wrong answers. Just write down the first thing you think of.)

1. salt and _____

2. burger and _____

3. read and _____

4. right and _____

5. night and _____

6. cake and _____

7. pen and _____

8. back and _____

9. apples and _____

10. listen and _____

Check to see if the person sitting next to you or other students in your class thought of the same things.

Directions: Choose the answer that best completes each analogy. The connection between the word pairs is *things or words that go together.* (**Hint:** Say the bolded words with the word *and* between them; for example, "cold *and* gray.")

1. **Safe** is to **sound** as **peace** is to _____.

   Ⓐ battle   Ⓒ noise

   Ⓑ quiet   Ⓓ protest

2. **Milk** is to **cream** as **sugar** is to _____.

   Ⓐ sweet   Ⓒ cane

   Ⓑ white   Ⓓ spice

3. **Odds** is to **ends** as **bits** is to _____.

   Ⓐ particles   Ⓒ pieces

   Ⓑ numbers   Ⓓ endings

4. **Rise** is to **shine** as **this** is to _____.

   Ⓐ there   Ⓒ that

   Ⓑ things   Ⓓ thus

5. **Give** is to **take** as **tried** is to _____.

   Ⓐ true   Ⓒ used

   Ⓑ donate   Ⓓ false

6. **Fast** is to **furious** as **life** is to _____.

   Ⓐ times   Ⓒ angry

   Ⓑ speedy   Ⓓ living

7. **Ups** is to **downs** as **hopes** is to _____.

   Ⓐ jumps   Ⓒ drums

   Ⓑ honest   Ⓓ dreams

8. **Now** is to **then** as **leaps** is to _____.

   Ⓐ years   Ⓒ future

   Ⓑ bounds   Ⓓ catches

Past and Present

A **verb** is an **action** word. A verb tells what you are doing. Verbs have different tenses: the **present** tense is for an action that is happening now, and the **past** tense is for an action that has already happened.

Directions: Look at the chart below. Write down two more examples using different verbs.

Present		Past	
Today I	bring	Yesterday I	brought
Today I	dance	Yesterday I	danced
Today I		Yesterday I	
Today I		Yesterday I	

Directions: Choose a word from the word box that best completes each analogy. (Be careful! Some of the words in the word box are not proper words.)

made	weeps	seal	take	flungs
maid	weeped	sell	taked	fling
making	wept	cell	tooks	flinged
spred	hurt	withstooded	finded	forget
spread	hurted	withstould	find	forgotten
spreaded	hert	withstood	found	forgots

1. discover : discovered :: find : _____

2. cry : cried :: weep : _____

3. purchased : purchase :: sold : _____

4. remembered : remember :: forgot : _____

5. create : created :: make : _____

6. tossed : toss :: flung : _____

7. returned : return :: took : _____

8. read : read :: hurt : _____

9. erode : eroded :: withstand : _____

10. upset : upset :: spread : _____

11. Write down the question numbers of the ones that were

   • present to past: _____   • synonyms: _____

   • past to present: _____   • antonyms: _____

   • impossible to tell: _____

Past and Present 2

Directions: These analogies are based on past and present verb tenses. Something past has already happened. Something present is now. Choose the answer that best completes each analogy. Pay attention to order, and watch out for spelling errors (for example, *builded* is not a word. The past tense of *build* is *built*.).

Hint: *Wound* is pronounced differently in questions 9 and 10. It rhymes with the word *sound* in question 9.

1. **write : wrote**
   - (A) present : past
   - (B) past : present

2. **wrote : write**
   - (A) present : past
   - (B) past : present

3. **skip : skipped**
   - (A) caught : catch
   - (C) crept : creep
   - (B) lent : lend
   - (D) lie : lay

4. **cried : cry**
   - (A) ski : skew
   - (C) flew : fly
   - (B) ski : skied
   - (D) flied : fly

5. **hear : heard**
   - (A) ate : eat
   - (C) slept : sleep
   - (B) go : went
   - (D) told : tell

6. **buy : bought**
   - (A) tore : tear
   - (C) sang : sing
   - (B) shut : shut
   - (D) ran : run

7. **stood : stand**
   - (A) tore : teared
   - (C) swam : swim
   - (B) tore : tored
   - (D) swimmed : swim

8. **think : thought**
   - (A) learn : learned
   - (C) studied : study
   - (B) taught : teach
   - (D) read : readed

9. **wind : wound**
   - (A) mind : mound
   - (C) hind : hound
   - (B) find : finded
   - (D) bind : bound

10. **wound : wounded**
    - (A) shone : shine
    - (C) ring : rang
    - (B) spun : spin
    - (D) left : leave

Directions: Fill in the blanks so the analogies are synonym pairs.

11. wound : injure :: heal : _____

12. wound : twisted :: _____ : untwist

13. wound (from #10) : tuned :: wound (from #9) : _____

Purpose

Directions: These analogies are based on a thing's purpose, or how it is used. Choose the answer that best completes each one. Be aware of order: | **nose : smell** | is not the same as | **smell : nose** |.

---

1. **nose : smell** is
   - Ⓐ thing : purpose
   - Ⓑ purpose : thing

2. **smell : nose** is
   - Ⓐ thing : purpose
   - Ⓑ purpose : thing

---

3. **pencil : draw :: elevator :**
   - Ⓐ protect
   - Ⓒ skyscraper
   - Ⓑ floor
   - Ⓓ transport

4. **scissors : cut :: microscope :**
   - Ⓐ shrink
   - Ⓒ magnify
   - Ⓑ filter
   - Ⓓ destroy

---

5. **scale : weigh**
   - Ⓐ telescope : spot
   - Ⓒ block : dam
   - Ⓑ observe : eye
   - Ⓓ bake : oven

6. **measure : ruler**
   - Ⓐ steer : rudder
   - Ⓒ needle : sew
   - Ⓑ hammer : pound
   - Ⓓ glass : window

---

7. **alarm : warn**
   - Ⓐ dig : shovel
   - Ⓒ catch : trap
   - Ⓑ taste : tongue
   - Ⓓ sieve : filter

8. **cut : saw**
   - Ⓐ fan : blow
   - Ⓒ mop : swab
   - Ⓑ sweep : broom
   - Ⓓ sponge : wipe

---

9. **shield : protect**
   - Ⓐ press : iron
   - Ⓒ tie : rope
   - Ⓑ read : book
   - Ⓓ arrow : pierce

10. **refrigerator : cool**
    - Ⓐ listen : radio
    - Ⓒ phone : talk
    - Ⓑ watch : television
    - Ⓓ sit : chair

Directions: Fill in the blanks to make your own analogies using the words in the word box. You may need to look up the words in a dictionary.

> thermometer   barometer   anemometer   hygrometer

11. _____ : _____ :: _____ : _____
        (thing)   *(use/purpose)*

12. _____ : _____ :: _____ : _____
      (use/purpose)   *(thing)*

Where Things Go

Some analogies are based on where things go, where they live, or where they're found.

Directions: Choose the answer that best completes each analogy.

Hint: Pay attention to order: | floor : carpet | is not the same as | carpet : floor |.

1. **floor : carpet**
   - Ⓐ thing : where goes
   - Ⓑ where goes : thing

2. **carpet : floor**
   - Ⓐ thing : where goes
   - Ⓑ where goes : thing

3. **goldfish : bowl**
   - Ⓐ elephant : tree
   - Ⓒ ocean : octopus
   - Ⓑ hamster : cage
   - Ⓓ gorilla : desert

4. **library : book**
   - Ⓐ table : kitchen
   - Ⓒ closet : shirt
   - Ⓑ letter : mailbox
   - Ⓓ cupboard : ice

5. **scarf : neck**
   - Ⓐ bracelet : wrist
   - Ⓒ necklace : ankle
   - Ⓑ feet : socks
   - Ⓓ finger : ring

6. **garage : car**
   - Ⓐ boat : dock
   - Ⓒ hangar : plane
   - Ⓑ train : station
   - Ⓓ cab : truck

7. **painting : gallery**
   - Ⓐ easel : artist
   - Ⓒ canal : boat
   - Ⓑ school : desk
   - Ⓓ artifact : museum

8. **movie : theater**
   - Ⓐ stage : play
   - Ⓒ cafeteria : eat
   - Ⓑ game : stadium
   - Ⓓ bike : pedal

9. **button : shirt**
   - Ⓐ handle : drawer
   - Ⓒ wheel : round
   - Ⓑ pants : zipper
   - Ⓓ wall : picture

10. **eel : ocean**
    - Ⓐ clam : tundra
    - Ⓒ seal : swamp
    - Ⓑ penguin : air
    - Ⓓ tortoise : desert

Directions: Complete the analogy using famous buildings, structures, or landmarks, and their locations. Your structures or landmarks can be natural or manmade.

11. _____ : _____ :: _____ : _____
    (landmark)   (location)   (landmark)   (location)

Animal Family Names

Directions: Some analogies are based on the names of old, young, male, female, and group family members. Choose the answer that best completes each analogy. Remember to pay attention to order.

Hint: A foal is a male or female baby horse.

---

1. **colt : filly** is
   - Ⓐ male foal : female foal
   - Ⓑ female foal : male foal

2. **filly : colt** is
   - Ⓐ male foal : female foal
   - Ⓑ female foal : male foal

---

3. **stallion : horse**
   - Ⓐ pig : boar
   - Ⓑ duck : drake
   - Ⓒ goose : gander
   - Ⓓ buck : antelope

4. **elephant : calf**
   - Ⓐ bull : cow
   - Ⓑ gosling : goose
   - Ⓒ fawn : deer
   - Ⓓ cat : kitten

---

5. **gull : colony**
   - Ⓐ flock : pigeon
   - Ⓑ wolf : pack
   - Ⓒ litter : pup
   - Ⓓ herd : buffalo

6. **fawn : doe**
   - Ⓐ lioness : cub
   - Ⓑ piglet : boar
   - Ⓒ foal : stallion
   - Ⓓ chick : hen

---

7. **ram : sheep**
   - Ⓐ cob : swan
   - Ⓑ whale : bull
   - Ⓒ pig : boar
   - Ⓓ egg : hen

8. **pride : lion**
   - Ⓐ dolphin : pod
   - Ⓑ fish : school
   - Ⓒ murder : crow
   - Ⓓ sheep : flock

---

9. **ewe : lamb**
   - Ⓐ cub : tigress
   - Ⓑ calf : moose
   - Ⓒ leopardess : cub
   - Ⓓ pup : seal

10. **kit : fox**
    - Ⓐ chick : ostrich
    - Ⓑ stallion : zebra
    - Ⓒ bull : elephant
    - Ⓓ duck : duckling

Directions: Use animal names to complete the analogies correctly.

Hint: Spiders are not insects. They are arachnids.

11. arachnid : insect :: _____ : _____

12. six legs : eight legs :: _____ : _____

Finding the Connection

Directions: Answer the analogies. Then write down the connection between the word pairs.

---

1. **peanut : shell**
- Ⓐ rind : melon
- Ⓑ peel : orange
- Ⓒ bark : tree
- Ⓓ pea : pod

2. **sparrow : feather**
- Ⓐ porcupine : quill
- Ⓑ fur : beaver
- Ⓒ wool : sheep
- Ⓓ scale : snake

3. **clam : shell**
- Ⓐ fur : wolf
- Ⓑ alligator : hide
- Ⓒ plate : armadillo
- Ⓓ shell : tortoise

---

4. What is the connection in #1–3? _____

5. Now, write a different word pair that has the same connection.

_____ : _____

---

6. **milk : carton**
- Ⓐ jar : jam
- Ⓑ bank : money
- Ⓒ letter : envelope
- Ⓓ teapot : tea

7. **feather : pillow**
- Ⓐ air : balloon
- Ⓑ canteen : water
- Ⓒ bowl : soup
- Ⓓ flower pot : dirt

8. **picture : album**
- Ⓐ sandbag : sand
- Ⓑ museum : art
- Ⓒ vase : flower
- Ⓓ pliers : toolbox

---

9. What is the connection in #6–8? _____

10. Now, write a different word pair that has the same connection.

_____ : _____

---

11. **water : canal**
- Ⓐ space : rocket
- Ⓑ current : wire
- Ⓒ wind : kite
- Ⓓ speaker : sound

12. **oil : pipeline**
- Ⓐ road : car
- Ⓑ track : train
- Ⓒ water : hose
- Ⓓ playground : child

13. **blood : vein**
- Ⓐ bottle : ketchup
- Ⓑ grape : vine
- Ⓒ leaf : branch
- Ⓓ sap : tree

---

14. What is the connection in #11–13? _____

15. Now, write a different word pair that has the same connection.

_____ : _____

Finding the Connection 2

Directions: Answer the analogies. Then write down the connection between the word pairs.

---

1. **man : lungs**
   - Ⓐ elephant : trunk
   - Ⓑ pig : snout
   - Ⓒ boy : breathe
   - Ⓓ fish : gills

2. **eagle : talon**
   - Ⓐ lion : mane
   - Ⓑ lion : claw
   - Ⓒ lion : fur
   - Ⓓ lion : wing

3. **elephant : tusk**
   - Ⓐ zebra : stripes
   - Ⓑ giraffe : neck
   - Ⓒ cobra : fang
   - Ⓓ leopard : spots

---

4. What is the connection in #1–3? _____

5. Now, write a different word pair that has the same connection.

   _____ : _____

---

6. **beak : parrot**
   - Ⓐ dog : muzzle
   - Ⓑ pig : snout
   - Ⓒ moose : nostril
   - Ⓓ mouth : mouse

7. **tentacle : squid**
   - Ⓐ starfish : arm
   - Ⓑ arm : octopus
   - Ⓒ whale : tail
   - Ⓓ shark : fin

8. **flipper : dolphin**
   - Ⓐ foreleg : horse
   - Ⓑ crow : wing
   - Ⓒ camel : hump
   - Ⓓ gorilla : arm

---

9. What is the connection in #6–8? _____

10. Now, write a different word pair that has the same connection.

    _____ : _____

---

11. **actress : actor**
    - Ⓐ host : hostess
    - Ⓑ steward : stewardess
    - Ⓒ waitress : waiter
    - Ⓓ god : goddess

12. **madam : sir**
    - Ⓐ king : queen
    - Ⓑ duke : duchess
    - Ⓒ lady : knight
    - Ⓓ prince : princess

13. **sister : brother**
    - Ⓐ aunt : uncle
    - Ⓑ nephew : niece
    - Ⓒ boy : girl
    - Ⓓ father : mother

---

14. What is the connection in #11–13? _____

15. Now, write a different word pair that has the same connection.

    _____ : _____

Finding the Connection 3

Directions: Answer the analogies. Then write down the connection between the word pairs.

---

1. **teacher : school**
   - (A) kitchen : cook
   - (B) actor : stage
   - (C) plane : pilot
   - (D) train : engineer

2. **judge : court**
   - (A) office : secretary
   - (B) studio : artist
   - (C) doctor : hospital
   - (D) store : clerk

3. **lifeguard : pool**
   - (A) track : runner
   - (B) field : farmer
   - (C) lab : scientist
   - (D) umpire : game

4. What is the connection in #1–3? _____

5. Now, write an analogy that has the same connection.

   _____ : _____

---

6. **float : jellyfish**
   - (A) slither : snake
   - (B) fly : ostrich
   - (C) pounce : deer
   - (D) soar : buffalo

7. **roar : lion**
   - (A) hen : cluck
   - (B) donkey : bray
   - (C) hiss : snake
   - (D) goat : bleat

8. **scurry : mouse**
   - (A) nut : squirrel
   - (B) march : ant
   - (C) beaver : gnaw
   - (D) kangaroo : jump

9. What is the connection in #6–8? _____

10. Now, write an analogy that has the same connection.

    _____ : _____

---

11. **tick : dog**
    - (A) barnacle : whale
    - (B) whisker : cat
    - (C) stripe : zebra
    - (D) mane : lion

12. **stamp : envelope**
    - (A) picture : book
    - (B) sand : beach
    - (C) flag : wave
    - (D) decal : car

13. **tack : board**
    - (A) pin : cushion
    - (B) glue : eat
    - (C) scissors : cut
    - (D) paper : staple

14. What is the connection in #11–13? _____

15. Now, write an analogy that has the same connection.

    _____ : _____

Trying Out the Connection

Directions: Write out how the word pairs are connected.

1. **swing : playground**
   - A _s_____ is located in a _p_____.

2. **mingle : blend**
   - If you _m_____ something, you _b_____ it.

3. **period : punctuation**
   - A _p_____ is a kind of _p_____.

Directions: Fill in the words to see which word pair is the correct answer (it will be the only one that makes sense). Then circle the correct answer.

4. **swing : playground**
   - Ⓐ pool : swimmer
   - Ⓑ rink : skater
   - Ⓒ caboose : highway
   - Ⓓ book : library
   - A _p_____ is located in a _s_____.
   - A _r_____ is located in a _s_____.
   - A _c_____ is located in a _h_____.
   - A _b_____ is located in a _l_____.

5. **mingle : blend**
   - Ⓐ complex : simple
   - Ⓑ hibernate : wake
   - Ⓒ observe : examine
   - Ⓓ ranger : park
   - If you _c_____ something, you _s_____ it.
   - If you _h_____ something, you _w_____ it.
   - If you _o_____ something, you _e_____ it.
   - If you _r_____ something, you _p_____ it.

6. **period : punctuation**
   - Ⓐ saxophone : instrument
   - Ⓑ cottage : palace
   - Ⓒ walnut : feather
   - Ⓓ computer : person
   - A _s_____ is a kind of _i_____.
   - A _c_____ is a kind of _p_____.
   - A _w_____ is a kind of _f_____.
   - A _c_____ is a kind of _p_____.

Part to Whole

Some word pairs in analogies are connected by *part to whole* or *whole to part*.

- **Examples:** letter : word (*part to whole*)

  word : letter (*whole to part*)

Directions: Choose the answer that best completes each analogy and answer the questions.

1. **word : sentence**
- (A) sentence : paragraph
- (B) sentence : vowel
- (C) report : sentence
- (D) story : sentence

2. **month : week**
- (A) icing : cake
- (B) time : watch
- (C) hour : minute
- (D) year : birthday

3. **spoke : wheel**
- (A) cage : bar
- (B) brush : bristle
- (C) ladder : step
- (D) tooth : comb

4. **star : constellation**
- (A) orbit : comet
- (B) planet : solar system
- (C) moon : Saturn
- (D) galaxy : black hole

5. **flower : petal**
- (A) chimney : brick
- (B) log : cabin
- (C) block : tower
- (D) wall : room

6. **note : scale**
- (A) letter : envelope
- (B) letter : alphabet
- (C) letter : mail
- (D) letter : cursive

7. **orchestra : musician**
- (A) athlete : strong
- (B) class : student
- (C) flute : blow
- (D) tree : forest

8. **book : chapter**
- (A) scene : movie
- (B) song : concert
- (C) play : act
- (D) step : dance

9. **strand : rope**
- (A) neck : necklace
- (B) jewelry : necklace
- (C) ring : necklace
- (D) bead : necklace

10. **bookcase : shelf**
- (A) room : house
- (B) stake : fence
- (C) library : read
- (D) dresser : drawer

11. **cake : slice**
- (A) corn : kernel
- (B) pat : butter
- (C) skin : apple
- (D) chip : potato

12. **camel : caravan**
- (A) fleet : ship
- (B) airplane : wing
- (C) boxcar : train
- (D) pack : dog

13. List the questions that were . . .

- part to whole: ____1____, _____   • whole to part: _____

14. Write your own analogy using four of these words or phrases: **pitcher**, **net**, **baseball team**, **plate**, **soccer team**, **forward**.

_____ : _____ :: _____ : _____

Is your analogy *part to whole* or *whole to part*? _____

Less Than/More Than

Some analogies are based on "less than" or "more than." One word in the word pair might be smaller, bigger, or not as strong or intense as the other word.

Directions: Choose the answer that best completes each analogy. (Remember to pay attention to order: **starved : hungry** is not the same as **hungry : starved**.)

---

1. starved : hungry is

- (A) less than : more than
- (B) more than : less than

2. hungry : starved is

- (A) less than : more than
- (B) more than : less than

---

3. glance : stare

- (A) pant : breathe
- (B) bawl : cry
- (C) ask : plead
- (D) shout : talk

4. scrub : wipe

- (A) gust : breeze
- (B) mischievous : evil
- (C) snack : feast
- (D) nip : bite

5. drip : gush

- (A) order : tell
- (B) nudge : shove
- (C) guzzle : sip
- (D) bang : tap

---

6. ancient : old

- (A) teensy : small
- (B) sprinkle : spray
- (C) giggle : laugh
- (D) skim : study

7. squabble : battle

- (A) pound : hit
- (B) silly : ridiculous
- (C) leap : hop
- (D) magnificent : good

8. tire : exhaust

- (A) slam : shut
- (B) ruin : harm
- (C) run : jog
- (D) moisten : drench

---

9. whisper : yell

- (A) freeze : cool
- (B) race : stroll
- (C) dip : soak
- (D) hurl : toss

10. ordinary : super

- (A) gorgeous : pretty
- (B) gigantic : big
- (C) brilliant : smart
- (D) tepid : boiling

11. terrify : startle

- (A) glimpse : observe
- (B) whisper : yell
- (C) adore : like
- (D) argue : fight

Directions: Make your own analogy where one word in the word pair is bigger, smaller, stronger, or more intense than the other word. If you want, you may use phrases instead of single words.

_____ : _____ :: _____ : _____

Classifying Analogies

Some analogies are based on how things can be grouped, or how they can be classified.

Directions: Fill in the blanks and choose the answer that best completes each analogy.

1. How are carrots and potatoes alike?
   - They are both kinds of ___v_____.

2. How are tables and chairs alike?
   - They are both kinds of ___f_____.

Hint: Pay attention to order: | **carrot : vegetable** | is not the same as | **vegetable : carrot** | !

A *carrot* is always a *vegetable*, but a *vegetable* is not always a *carrot*. So, | **table : furniture** |
is not the same as | **furniture : table** |.

3. A ___t_____ is always a piece of _____.
   A piece of _____ is not always a _____.

---

4. **Everest : mountain**
   - (A) Nile : Amazon
   - (B) Amazon : Nile
   - (C) Nile : river
   - (D) river : Nile

5. **color : scarlet**
   - (A) rose : flower
   - (B) flower : rose
   - (C) white : daisy
   - (D) daisy : white

6. **pepper : spice**
   - (A) quartz : mineral
   - (B) mineral : quartz
   - (C) salt : cinnamon
   - (D) cinnamon : salt

7. **Juneau : capital**
   - (A) Paris : London
   - (B) London : Paris
   - (C) country : Mexico
   - (D) Mexico : country

8. **organ : heart**
   - (A) leg : limb
   - (B) limb : leg
   - (C) finger : hand
   - (D) hand : finger

9. **sandal : shoe**
   - (A) boot : sneaker
   - (B) sneaker : boot
   - (C) iron : metal
   - (D) metal : iron

10. **punctuation : comma**
    - (A) appliance : stove
    - (B) stove : appliance
    - (C) cool : refrigerator
    - (D) refrigerator : cool

11. **apple : fruit**
    - (A) orange : banana
    - (B) banana : orange
    - (C) grain : wheat
    - (D) wheat : grain

12. **weapon : cannon**
    - (A) panther : cat
    - (B) cat : panther
    - (C) lion : leopard
    - (D) leopard : lion

Challenge:

- Name a place that is always a country and a continent. _____
- Name a place that is always a country but not always a continent. _____

Classifying Analogies 2

Directions: Fill in the blanks and choose the answer that best completes each analogy.

1. How are a poodle and a Saint Bernard alike?

   • They are both d_____.

2. Why are these word pairs different? | poodle : dog | | dog : poodle |

   • A p_____ is always a _____.

   • A d_____ is not always a _____.

---

3. **screwdriver : tool**
   - Ⓐ boat : canoe
   - Ⓑ kayak : boat
   - Ⓒ carrot : fruit
   - Ⓓ fruit : pear

4. **desert : Sahara**
   - Ⓐ cactus : plant
   - Ⓑ sedimentary : rock
   - Ⓒ ocean : Pacific
   - Ⓓ Ganges : river

5. **mouse : rodent**
   - Ⓐ salmon : fish
   - Ⓑ feline : cheetah
   - Ⓒ bird : vulture
   - Ⓓ canine : collie

6. **violin : instrument**
   - Ⓐ amphibian : frog
   - Ⓑ mammal : giraffe
   - Ⓒ insect : locust
   - Ⓓ crocodile : reptile

7. **Mercury : planet**
   - Ⓐ candy : lollipop
   - Ⓑ star : Sun
   - Ⓒ clothes : shirt
   - Ⓓ hip hop : music

8. **haiku : poem**
   - Ⓐ flower : tulip
   - Ⓑ book : novel
   - Ⓒ redwood : tree
   - Ⓓ cheese : cheddar

9. **game : basketball**
   - Ⓐ Russia : continent
   - Ⓑ island : Madagascar
   - Ⓒ Africa : country
   - Ⓓ ocean : Caribbean

10. **van : vehicle**
    - Ⓐ femur : bone
    - Ⓑ color : crimson
    - Ⓒ dog : poodle
    - Ⓓ falls : Niagara

11. **month : October**
    - Ⓐ Friday : day
    - Ⓑ season : spring
    - Ⓒ year : century
    - Ⓓ week : seven

Directions: Write your own answer choices. Make sure only one answer choice is correct. On the lines to the right, tell which answer is correct and why.

12. | beverage : orange juice | **Explanation**

    Ⓐ _____ : dessert   _____

    Ⓑ dessert : _____   _____

    Ⓒ _____ : dessert   _____

    Ⓓ dessert : _____   _____

Practice Making Classes

Similar kinds of things can be grouped by category or class. For example, a rose can be classified as a flower. It is a member of the flower group.

Directions: Think of the names of as many items as you can that fit in each given group or class.

Class	Class Members or Items
1. fabrics	
2. machines	
3. governments	
4. games and/or sports	
5. vocalists (singers)	
6. explorers	

Directions: Write two analogy questions using class names and some of the things you listed as members of each class. One question should have the class name first, then an item. One question should have an item first, and then the class name.

7. _____ : _____

    Ⓐ _____ : _____

    Ⓑ _____ : _____

    Ⓒ _____ : _____

    Ⓓ _____ : _____

Correct answer: _____

Is your answer *class to member* or *member to class*? _____

8. _____ : _____

    Ⓐ _____ : _____

    Ⓑ _____ : _____

    Ⓒ _____ : _____

    Ⓓ _____ : _____

Correct answer: _____

Is your answer *class to member* or *member to class*? _____

Multiple-Meaning Words

Some words have more than one meaning. For example, the word *burn* can be a noun or a verb.

- A **noun** is a person, place or thing. (I have a <u>burn</u> on my hand.)
- A **verb** is an action word. (Learn the code, and then <u>burn</u> it.)

Directions: Pick which answer choice best completes each analogy.

1. <u>Paper</u> the message on the wall. : I read your <u>paper</u>.

   Ⓐ noun : verb   Ⓑ verb : noun

2. I did not <u>soil</u> my shirt. : Crops will thrive in this <u>soil</u>.

   Ⓐ noun : verb   Ⓑ verb : noun

3. My tire needs a <u>patch</u>. : I will <u>patch</u> my tire tomorrow.

   Ⓐ noun : verb   Ⓑ verb : noun

4. Here is a <u>list</u> of names. : Will you <u>list</u> the names?

   Ⓐ noun : verb   Ⓑ verb : noun

5. Don't <u>spy</u> on your sister! : No one knew who the <u>spy</u> was.

   Ⓐ noun : verb   Ⓑ verb : noun

6. The <u>map</u> needs to be redrawn. : I will <u>map</u> out the route.

   Ⓐ noun : verb   Ⓑ verb : noun

7. My <u>hope</u> is to finish first. : I <u>hope</u> you finish first.

   Ⓐ noun : verb   Ⓑ verb : noun

8. Don't <u>paw</u> at my face! : My dog hurt its <u>paw</u>.

   Ⓐ noun : verb   Ⓑ verb : noun

9. <u>Oil</u> the bike chain. : <u>Oil</u> is an ingredient in salad dressing.

   Ⓐ noun : verb   Ⓑ verb : noun

10. I'll rest a <u>spell</u>. : I'll <u>spell</u> those words for you.

    Ⓐ noun : verb   Ⓑ verb : noun

Multiple-Meaning Words 2

Directions: Write out the connection between the word pair in the question. Then choose the answer that best completes each analogy. **(Hints:** Remember that some words have multiple meanings. Also, watch out for which word comes first in the word pair!)

---

1. guess : estimate
- Ⓐ bellow : whisper
- Ⓑ calm : excitement
- Ⓒ grumble : complaint
- Ⓓ courage : cowardice

     synonyms

2. guess : know
- Ⓐ confuse : enlighten
- Ⓑ decide : choose
- Ⓒ deceive : trick
- Ⓓ confine : restrict

3. staple : necessity
- Ⓐ sleeve : shirt
- Ⓑ stage : actor
- Ⓒ squeak : mouse
- Ⓓ extra : luxury

---

4. staple : fasten
- Ⓐ feast : starve
- Ⓑ start : commence
- Ⓒ steal : return
- Ⓓ forget : remember

5. master : learn
- Ⓐ contain : free
- Ⓑ electrify : bore
- Ⓒ maintain : end
- Ⓓ expel : remove

6. master : servant
- Ⓐ sailor : captain
- Ⓑ serf : lord
- Ⓒ teacher : pupil
- Ⓓ soldier : general

---

7. trade : profession
- Ⓐ legend : story
- Ⓑ braid : wig
- Ⓒ castle : shack
- Ⓓ cauldron : plate

8. trade : exchange
- Ⓐ fetch : accept
- Ⓑ imagine : pretend
- Ⓒ lead : follow
- Ⓓ preach : listen

9. talk : speech
- Ⓐ spoon : ladle
- Ⓑ fork : knife
- Ⓒ cup : drink
- Ⓓ plate : table

---

10. talk : utter
- Ⓐ lower : increase
- Ⓑ purify : clean
- Ⓒ disguise : reveal
- Ⓓ renew : stop

11. string : beads
- Ⓐ eat : cards
- Ⓑ watch : radios
- Ⓒ bend : dishes
- Ⓓ stack : blocks

12. string : rope
- Ⓐ truck : drive
- Ⓑ computer : type
- Ⓒ doormat : carpet
- Ⓓ dinner : evening

---

13. Write down two meanings for the word *share*.

_____

_____

14. Make an analogy with the word *share*.

_____ : _____ :: _____ : _____

Math

A mnemonic device is an aid that helps you remember something. Here is a common mnemonic for remembering the order in which to perform mathematical operations:

> **Pretty Please My Dear Aunt Sally**
> - **P**retty = Do what's in the **p**arentheses ( ) first!
> - **P**lease = Next do **p**owers, like 2^2!
> - **M**y **D**ear = Do **m**ultiplication and **d**ivision next, going from left to right.
> - **A**unt **S**ally: **A**ddition and **s**ubtraction are done last, also going from left to right.

Directions: Use the mnemonic to answer the analogies correctly. All questions will refer to this problem: $(5 + 4) \times 2^2 \div 3 - 7 + 2 =$

1. **Dear : division :: Please :**
   - Ⓐ multiplication
   - Ⓑ parentheses
   - Ⓒ subtraction
   - Ⓓ powers

2. **Aunt : Sally :: addition :**
   - Ⓐ subtraction
   - Ⓑ powers
   - Ⓒ multiplication
   - Ⓓ division

3. **x : ( ) :: my :**
   - Ⓐ please
   - Ⓑ dear
   - Ⓒ aunt
   - Ⓓ pretty

4. **x and ÷ : left to right :: + and − :**
   - Ⓐ right to left
   - Ⓑ left to right
   - Ⓒ right to right
   - Ⓓ left to left

5. **first : second :: (5 + 4) :**
   - Ⓐ $7 - 2$
   - Ⓑ 2^2
   - Ⓒ $3 + 7$
   - Ⓓ $\times 2^2$

6. **first : last :: (5 + 4) :**
   - Ⓐ $+ 7$
   - Ⓑ $- 7$
   - Ⓒ $+ 2$
   - Ⓓ $- 2$

7. **(5 + 4) x 4 : 5 + 4 x 4 :: 36 :**
   - Ⓐ 21
   - Ⓑ 26
   - Ⓒ 31
   - Ⓓ 36

8. **problem : solution :: $(5 + 4) \times 2^2 \div 3 - 7 + 2$:**
   - Ⓐ 5
   - Ⓑ 6
   - Ⓒ 7
   - Ⓓ 8

Challenge: Create four answer choices to complete the analogy below. Make sure only one answer is correct!

problem : solution :: _____ : _____

Ⓐ _____ : _____   Ⓒ _____ : _____

Ⓑ _____ : _____   Ⓓ _____ : _____

Math 2

Directions: Choose the answer that best completes each analogy.

Hint: To <u>m</u>ake a percent, <u>m</u>ultiply by 100%. (**Example:** .04 × 100 = 4%)
To <u>d</u>rop a percent, <u>d</u>ivide by 100%. (**Example:** 42% ÷ 100% = .42)

---

1. **1 : 4 :: 100% :**

   Ⓐ 4% Ⓑ 40% Ⓒ 400% Ⓓ 4000%

2. **.2 : .8 :: 20% :**

   Ⓐ .08% Ⓑ .8% Ⓒ 8% Ⓓ 80%

3. **40% : 60% :: .4 :**

   Ⓐ 60 Ⓑ .06 Ⓒ .6 Ⓓ 6.0

4. **25% : 2500% :: .25 :**

   Ⓐ 25 Ⓑ 250 Ⓒ 2.5 Ⓓ .025

5. **75% : 750% :: .75 :**

   Ⓐ 7.5 Ⓑ 75 Ⓒ 750 Ⓓ 7500

6. **50 : .5 :: 5,000% :**

   Ⓐ 5% Ⓑ 50% Ⓒ 500% Ⓓ 5,000%

7. **9 : .9 :: 900% :**

   Ⓐ .09% Ⓑ .9% Ⓒ 9% Ⓓ 90%

8. **110% : 1.1 :: 150% :**

   Ⓐ .15 Ⓑ 1.5 Ⓒ 15 Ⓓ 150

9. **222% : 2.22 :: 777% :**

   Ⓐ 777 Ⓑ 77 Ⓒ 7.7 Ⓓ 7.77

10. **400% : 4 :: 600% :**

    Ⓐ .06 Ⓑ .6 Ⓒ 6 Ⓓ 60

Directions: Use the answer choices to complete each analogy. Explain your reasoning.

11. **bigger : smaller ::** _____ : _____

    • Answer choices: **1% of the ocean** and **99% of a glass of water**

    • Explanation: _____

12. **smaller : bigger ::** _____ : _____

    • Answer choices: **1% of the forest** and **99% of one tree**

    • Explanation: _____

Social Studies

Directions: Find the word that best completes each analogy.

Hint: You may want to use an atlas or the Internet to find a detailed world map.

1. Washington, D.C. : United States :: Canberra : _____

2. Beijing : China :: Ottawa : _____

3. Baghdad : Iraq :: Mexico City : _____

4. Madrid : Spain :: Paris : _____

5. Ankara : Turkey :: Kabul : _____

6. Moscow : Russia :: London : _____

7. Lima : Peru :: Tokyo : _____

8. Nairobi : Kenya :: Buenos Aires : _____

9. Kingston : Jamaica :: New Delhi : _____

10. Vatican City : Vatican City :: Singapore : _____

11. Reykjavík : Iceland :: Copenhagen : _____

12. Brasília : Brazil :: Cairo : _____

Directions: Write analogies using different countries and capitals from the ones in the questions.

13. _____ : _____ :: _____ : _____

14. _____ : _____ :: _____ : _____

Challenge: Explain why one would have to be careful writing this type of analogy if one used the capitals of South Africa and Bolivia.

Social Studies 2

The analogies below are made from the names of the world's longest rivers.

Directions: Fill in the correct continent to complete each analogy. The number of times a continent is used is listed in the box below, but you may want to look at a map or the Internet to check your answers.

Africa — 2	**Australia — 1**	**North America — 2**
Asia — 4	**Europe — 1**	**South America — 2**

1. Yukon : North America :: Nile : _____

2. Yenisey : Asia :: Amazon : _____

3. Amur : Asia :: Chang Jiang (Yangtze) : _____

4. Lena : Asia :: Mississippi/Missouri : _____

5. Purus : South America :: Ob-Irtysh : _____

6. Shatt al-Arab-Euphrates : Asia :: Congo : _____

7. Salween : Asia :: Huang He (Yellow) : _____

8. Niger : Africa :: Rio de la Plata-Parana : _____

9. Indus : Asia :: Murray-Darling : _____

10. Madeira : South America :: Volga : _____

11. Sao Francisco : South America :: Mekong : _____

12. Syr Darya-Naryn : Asia :: Mackenzie : _____

Challenge: Name the continent that doesn't have a major river on it. Explain why.

_____

_____

Science

Directions: A Periodic Table of the Elements will help you choose the correct answer to complete each analogy.

Hint: Enter "periodic table" into an Internet search engine to find a suitable online resource.

1. **calendar : date :: periodic table :**
   (A) gas
   (B) molecule
   (C) element
   (D) metal

2. **Au : gold :: Ag :**
   (A) silver
   (B) copper
   (C) aluminum
   (D) nickel

3. **alkali metal : potassium :: noble gas :**
   (A) iodine
   (B) krypton
   (C) bromine
   (D) lithium

4. **He : helium :: Fe :**
   (A) radon
   (B) iron
   (C) xenon
   (D) tin

5. **1 : hydrogen :: 80 :**
   (A) chromium
   (B) silicon
   (C) helium
   (D) mercury

6. **halogen : chlorine :: non-metal :**
   (A) oxygen
   (B) calcium
   (C) cesium
   (D) radium

7. **Europium : 63 :: Einsteinium :**
   (A) 66
   (B) 77
   (C) 88
   (D) 99

8. **Nitrogen : N :: Carbon :**
   (A) Cr
   (B) Co
   (C) C
   (D) Cl

9. **metalloid : arsenic :: rare earth element :**
   (A) Germanium
   (B) Uranium
   (C) neon
   (D) Francium

10. **nitrogen : N :: sodium :**
    (A) Sn
    (B) S
    (C) Nb
    (D) Na

Challenge: Write down the names of the three elements whose numbers correspond to the following criteria:

11. The element whose number equals your age: _____

12. The element whose number is twice your age: _____

13. The element whose number is five times your grade level: _____

14. In how many years will your age equal Fermium's number? _____

Science 2

Directions: Use these words to answer the analogies below. Use each word twice.

producer	secondary consumer	decomposer
primary consumer	tertiary consumer	

Looking at the food chain diagram may help you figure out your answers. When you look at the first word pair in each question, think, "What eats what?" This will help you know where the word you fill in fits on the food chain.

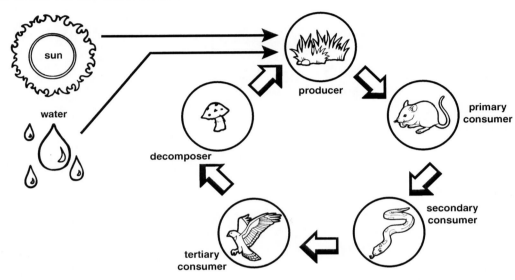

1. acorn : squirrel :: producer : _____

2. cow : person :: primary consumer : _____

3. spider : mushroom :: secondary consumer : _____

4. bear : berry :: primary consumer : _____

5. bear : insect :: secondary consumer : _____

6. penguin : orca :: secondary consumer : _____

7. rabbit : bacteria :: primary consumer : _____

8. small fish : algae :: primary consumer : _____

9. deer : wolverine : primary consumer : _____

10. big fish : eagle :: secondary consumer : _____

Challenge: Give an example of what a person might eat when he or she is a primary, secondary, and tertiary consumer.

• Primary: _____

• Secondary: _____

• Tertiary: _____

Skeleton Analogies

Directions: Use the skeleton to help you choose the answer that best completes each analogy.

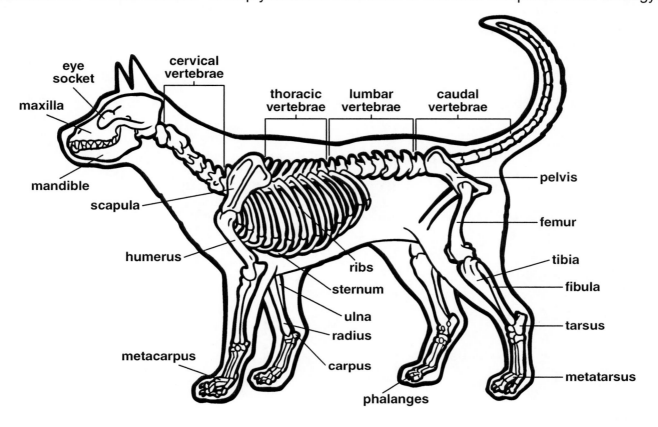

1. front leg : humerus :: back leg : _____

2. forepaw : metacarpus :: hindpaw : _____

3. ulna : radius :: fibula : _____

4. wrist : carpus :: ankle : _____

5. cervical vertebrae : neck :: caudal vertebrae : _____

6. shoulder blade : scapula :: breastbone : _____

7. ankle : toes :: tarsus : _____

8. upper jaw : lower jaw :: maxilla : _____

Challenge: Do you think a Great Dane has more bones than a Chihuahua? Tell why.

_____

_____

Spelling

Directions: Use the words below to answer the analogies correctly. Each word will be used twice. Be prepared to think hard, as these words are among the most commonly misspelled in the English language!

> **a lot** = a large amount or number
>
> **allot** = to divide, give out in shares
>
> **all together** = in a group
>
> **altogether** = entirely, completely, everything included
>
> **all ready** = all prepared; can be replaced by *ready*
>
> **already** = before, previously; cannot be replaced by *ready*

1. couple : two :: many : _____

2. by one's self : in a group :: solo : _____

3. after : following :: previously : _____

4. join : unite :: divide : _____

5. largely : mostly :: entirely : _____

6. not prepared : not ready :: prepared to go : _____

7. puddle : ocean :: a little : _____

8. add in : combine :: give out in shares : _____

9. tired out : not ready :: warmed up : _____

10. separate : apart :: included : _____

11. apart : bunched :: alone : _____

12. later : afterward :: before : _____

Challenge: Fill in the following sentences with *all together* or *altogether.*

- We were _____ at the party.

- _____ it cost 50 dollars.

Homophones

Homophones are words that sound alike. Homophones are not synonyms, and they are not spelled the same.

Directions: Give three reasons why *thrown* and *throne* are homophones.

1. _____

2. _____

3. _____

Directions: Pick the correct homophone from the word box to complete each analogy. If you are not sure of what some of the words mean, check their meanings in a dictionary.

stationary	pier	sight	site	their
stationery	peer	cite	they're	there

1. nose : smell :: eye : _____

2. a superior : boss :: an equal : _____

3. traveling : moving :: still : _____

4. house : home :: place : _____

5. she owns it : her :: they own it : _____

6. she is : she's :: they are : _____

7. timepiece : watch :: paper : _____

8. harbor : port :: wharf : _____

9. close : here :: farther away : _____

10. review : view :: recite : _____

Directions: Write the words *paper*, *stationary*, and *stationery* in the boxes below. Then, circle the *er* in paper. Also circle the *er* in the other word you wrote that is a type of paper used for letter writing.

Homophones 2

Homophones are words that sound alike. Homophones are not spelled the same, and they have different meanings.

Directions: Why are *weight* and *wait* homophones? Include their definitions in your answer.

_____

_____

Directions: Pick the correct homophone from the word box to complete each analogy.

weather	whether	idle	idol	allowed	aloud	it's	its

1. not awake : asleep :: not working : _____

2. belonging to him : his :: belonging to it : _____

3. atmosphere : air :: climate : _____

4. outlaw : villain :: hero : _____

5. unspoken : spoken :: silent : _____

6. for sure : definitely :: in either case : _____

7. he is : he's :: it is : _____

8. prevent : banned :: permit : _____

Directions: Rewrite the sentences, changing the word order, so that they make sense.

9. Ice cream for I scream. _____

10. Lettuce eat let us. _____

Think and Write: Explain why spelling is important, even if one has a spell check on a computer. Use an example of a homophone pair in your answer.

_____

_____

All Things Time

Civilian, or regular time, uses the numbers 1 to 12 to identify each of the 24 hours in a day. The letters "A.M." and "P.M." are used to identify the hours before and after midnight. In *military* time, the hours are numbered from 00 to 23.

Directions: Use the following examples to help you complete the analogies.

	Midnight			**Noon**		
Civilian Time	12:00 A.M.	3:30 A.M.	9:45 A.M.	12:00 P.M.	3:30 P.M.	9:45 P.M.
Military Time	0000	0330	0945	1200	1530	2145

1. **typical school start : typical school end**

   Ⓐ 1600 : 2200   Ⓑ 2200 : 1600   Ⓒ 0830 : 1530   Ⓓ 1530 : 0830

2. **movie begins early evening : ends 2 hours later**

   Ⓐ 1830 : 2030   Ⓑ 2030 : 1830   Ⓒ 0630 : 0830   Ⓓ 0830 : 0630

3. **afternoon tea : brunch**

   Ⓐ 2130 : 2300   Ⓑ 2300 : 2130   Ⓒ 1030 : 1400   Ⓓ 1400 : 1030

4. **breakfast : lunch**

   Ⓐ 1145 : 0700   Ⓑ 0700 : 1145   Ⓒ 0630 : 0000   Ⓓ 0000 : 0630

5. **plane flies through the night : lands early morning**

   Ⓐ 0400 : 2215   Ⓑ 2215 : 0400   Ⓒ 1255 : 1720   Ⓓ 1720 : 1255

6. **begins work late afternoon : works 8-hour shift**

   Ⓐ 0800 : 1600   Ⓑ 1600 : 0800   Ⓒ 1500 : 2300   Ⓓ 2300 : 1500

7. **phone call middle of the night : talks for 70 minutes**

   Ⓐ 1420 : 1300   Ⓑ 1300 : 1520   Ⓒ 0510 : 0400   Ⓓ 0230 : 0340

8. **concert begins after lunch : ends before dinner**

   Ⓐ 2100 : 1830   Ⓑ 1830 : 2100   Ⓒ 1430 : 1700   Ⓓ 1700 : 1430

9. **wakes up after nightmare : goes back to sleep 40 minutes later**

   Ⓐ 0020 : 2340   Ⓑ 2340 : 0020   Ⓒ 0030 : 0430   Ⓓ 0430 : 0030

10. **surgery begins : operation ends 7 hours later**

    Ⓐ 0830 : 1530   Ⓑ 1530 : 0830   Ⓒ 1615 : 0915   Ⓓ 0915 : 1715

Challenge: Space programs—as well as many police, hospital, rescue, and other emergency-service departments—use military time. Tell why you think so.

_____

_____

Fearful Analogies

Directions: Don't be afraid! If you use the chart, you will be able to complete the analogies correctly. A phobia is a very strong and unreasonable fear.

Phobia	Fear of	Phobia	Fear of
claustrophobia	closed spaces	pyrophobia	fire
astrophobia	lightning	ichthyophobia	fish
agoraphobia	open spaces	logophobia	study
brontophobia	thunder	dermatophobia	skin
entomophobia	insects	graphophobia	writing

1. **elevator : claustrophobia**
- Ⓐ brontophobia : storm
- Ⓑ logophobia : study
- Ⓒ beetle : dermatophobia
- Ⓓ salmon : icthyophobia

2. **agoraphobia : field**
- Ⓐ entomophobia : rash
- Ⓑ claustrophobia : plain
- Ⓒ pyrophobia : campfire
- Ⓓ lightning : astrophobia

3. **graphophobia : report**
- Ⓐ pyrophobia : water
- Ⓑ logophobia : test
- Ⓒ astrophobia : star
- Ⓓ brontophobia : silence

4. **trout : icthyophobia**
- Ⓐ bee : entomophobia
- Ⓑ badger : entomophobia
- Ⓒ bat : entomophobia
- Ⓓ bird : entomophobia

5. **agoraphobia : open water**
- Ⓐ claustrophobia : trail
- Ⓑ claustrophobia : bridge
- Ⓒ claustrophobia : road
- Ⓓ claustrophobia : tunnel

6. **reading : logophobia**
- Ⓐ shedding : dermatophobia
- Ⓑ singing : ichthyophobia
- Ⓒ swimming : graphophobia
- Ⓓ sewing : pyrophobia

7. **pyrophobia : match**
- Ⓐ agoraphobia : cave
- Ⓑ agoraphobia : prairie
- Ⓒ agoraphobia : closet
- Ⓓ agoraphobia : shed

8. **ant : entomophobia**
- Ⓐ dog : icthyophobia
- Ⓑ grandmother : pyrophobia
- Ⓒ bolt : astrophobia
- Ⓓ brontophobia : thunder

9. What do you think the following scientists study?

- entomologists: _____
- ichthyologists: _____

10. If *calli* is a Greek root meaning "beautiful," what is the meaning of the word *calligraphy*?

_____

Inventions of the Century

Directions: In what century were these useful items invented? Find out and complete the analogies. Here are some helpful hints:

- The 12th century contains the years 1101–1200.
- The 21st century contains the years 2001–2100.

---

1. **small pox vaccine (1796) : pop-up toaster (1927) ::**

    (A) 17th : 20th   (B) 17th : 21st   (C) 18th : 21st   (D) 18th : 20th

2. **bar code system (1970) : zipper (1891) ::**

    (A) 20th : 19th   (B) 19th : 20th   (C) 19th : 18th   (D) 18th : 19th

3. **belt-driven spinning wheel (1280) : blood groups (1901) ::**

    (A) 12th : 20th   (B) 12th : 21st   (C) 13th : 20th   (D) 13th : 21st

4. **+ and – math signs (1489) : x math sign (1631) ::**

    (A) 15th : 17th   (B) 15th : 16th   (C) 14th : 17th   (D) 14th : 16th

5. **hot-air balloon (1782) : first parachute jump (1797) ::**

    (A) 18th : 19th   (B) 18th : 18th   (C) 17th : 19th   (D) 17th : 17th

6. **magnifying glass (1250) : eyeglasses (1285) ::**

    (A) 11th : 11th   (B) 12th : 12th   (C) 13th : 13th   (D) 14th : 14th

7. **cast iron pipe (1455) : passenger elevator (1857) ::**

    (A) 14th : 18th   (B) 14th : 19th   (C) 15th : 18th   (D) 15th : 19th

8. **portable clock (1500) : paper clip (1900) ::**

    (A) 14th : 19th   (B) 15th : 19th   (C) 14th : 20th   (D) 15th : 20th

9. **artificial heart (1982) : steam engine (1712) ::**

    (A) 19th : 17th   (B) 19th : 18th   (C) 20th : 17th   (D) 20th : 18th

10. **graphite pencil (1565) : ballpoint pen (1938) ::**

    (A) 16th : 20th   (B) 16th : 19th   (C) 15th : 20th   (D) 15th : 19th

---

Challenge: Using the information on this page, write why skyscrapers were more likely to be built after 1857 than before.

_____

_____

Review of Analogy Types

Directions: Choose the answer that best completes each analogy. Write **synonym**, **antonym**, **plural**, **adjective**, **what people use**, or **past/present** on the blank line to describe how the question and answer words are connected. There will be two of each kind of analogy. Remember to pay attention to order, and remember that there can only be one right answer!

1. **cobra : poisonous**
- Ⓐ shirt : sleeve
- Ⓑ cotton : skirt
- Ⓒ jacket : zipper
- Ⓓ jeans : denim

_____

2. **study : frolic**
- Ⓐ educate : teach
- Ⓑ subtract : add
- Ⓒ smile : grin
- Ⓓ strut : swagger

_____

3. **forgave : forgive**
- Ⓐ broke : break
- Ⓑ feed : fed
- Ⓒ bring : brought
- Ⓓ feel : felt

_____

4. **revolting : gross**
- Ⓐ silly : somber
- Ⓑ soiled : clean
- Ⓒ elegant : tasteful
- Ⓓ extended : short

_____

5. **referee : whistle**
- Ⓐ saw : carpenter
- Ⓑ sculptor : chisel
- Ⓒ axe : logger
- Ⓓ hoe : gardener

_____

6. **goose : geese**
- Ⓐ kitten : cat
- Ⓑ feet : foot
- Ⓒ cubs : bear
- Ⓓ mouse : mice

_____

7. **porch : veranda**
- Ⓐ deck : wood
- Ⓑ task : gift
- Ⓒ jewel : gemstone
- Ⓓ brick : patio

_____

8. **beam : wooden**
- Ⓐ cat : paw
- Ⓑ giraffe : neck
- Ⓒ dog : faithful
- Ⓓ striped : tiger

_____

9. **pole : skier**
- Ⓐ rolling pin : chef
- Ⓑ cat : mouse
- Ⓒ blanket : bed
- Ⓓ boxer : gloves

_____

10. **pants : pants**
- Ⓐ socks : sock
- Ⓑ button : buttons
- Ⓒ shoes : shoe
- Ⓓ zippers : zipper

_____

11. **inquire : answer**
- Ⓐ increase : add
- Ⓑ work : toil
- Ⓒ find : treasure
- Ⓓ melt : solidify

_____

12. **hit : hit**
- Ⓐ had : have
- Ⓑ grow : grew
- Ⓒ sell : sold
- Ⓓ rise : rose

_____

13. Why did you have to eliminate answer choices to find the correct answer for #10 and #12?

_____

Review of Analogy Types 2

Directions: Choose the answer that best completes each analogy. Write **homophone**, **less than/more than**, **member to group**, **purpose**, **male/female**, or **where found** on the blank line to describe how the question and answer words are connected. There will be two of each kind of analogy. Remember to pay attention to order!

---

1. **flannel : fabric**
   - Ⓐ lizard : reptile
   - Ⓑ mammal : squirrel
   - Ⓒ bird : starling
   - Ⓓ plant : fern

2. **simmer : boil**
   - Ⓐ gallop : walk
   - Ⓑ pour : drip
   - Ⓒ sip : gulp
   - Ⓓ dehydrate : dry

3. **fourth : forth**
   - Ⓐ quarter : coin
   - Ⓑ sore : soar
   - Ⓒ whom : who's
   - Ⓓ dough : bread

4. **cowboy : ranch**
   - Ⓐ botanist : plant
   - Ⓑ astronaut : pilot
   - Ⓒ mine : miner
   - Ⓓ lifeguard : beach

5. **hatchet : chop**
   - Ⓐ kite : tail
   - Ⓑ blow : horn
   - Ⓒ roof : cover
   - Ⓓ shave : razor

6. **road : rowed**
   - Ⓐ strait : straight
   - Ⓑ channel : water
   - Ⓒ bend : twist
   - Ⓓ sing : sang

7. **stallion : mare**
   - Ⓐ lioness : lion
   - Ⓑ ewe : ram
   - Ⓒ cow : bull
   - Ⓓ rooster : hen

8. **prince : princess**
   - Ⓐ mistress : master
   - Ⓑ countess : count
   - Ⓒ dame : sir
   - Ⓓ duke : duchess

9. **director : set**
   - Ⓐ track : runner
   - Ⓑ hiker : trail
   - Ⓒ stage : actress
   - Ⓓ barracks : soldier

10. **tremble : shake**
    - Ⓐ freeze : chill
    - Ⓑ adore : like
    - Ⓒ smell : stink
    - Ⓓ bully : tease

11. **hockey : sport**
    - Ⓐ salt : spice
    - Ⓑ poem : sonnet
    - Ⓒ planet : Mars
    - Ⓓ flower : daffodil

12. **tweezers : pluck**
    - Ⓐ protect : helmet
    - Ⓑ pump : inflate
    - Ⓒ weigh : scale
    - Ⓓ transport : taxi

---

13. If the wrong answers for questions 8, 9, 10, 11, and 12 had been written in a different order, would they have been correct? Write "yes" or "no" for each one.

#8 _____   #9 _____   #10 _____   #11 _____   #12 _____

Use What You Know

Sometimes you may not know a word, or the word may have a different meaning than you are familiar with. Don't give up! Sometimes you can figure out the answer by using what you know.

Directions: Go through the answer choices. Write down how the words you know are connected. Cross out the ones that do not have the same connection as the words in the question. The correct answer will be the one that is not crossed out.

Connection

1. **loyal : unfaithful** _____antonyms_____

   Ⓐ basketball : sport _____not antonyms, member to group_____

   Ⓑ fashionable : stylish _____

   Ⓒ pedestrian : exciting _____?????_____

   Ⓓ fax machine : send _____

2. **Most likely, when something is *pedestrian*, it is**

   Ⓐ unfriendly, not welcoming.   Ⓒ not dull, exciting.

   Ⓑ friendly, welcoming.   Ⓓ dull, unexciting.

Connection

3. **tale : story** _____

   Ⓐ conundrum : riddle _____?????_____

   Ⓑ rim : center _____

   Ⓒ needle : sew _____

   Ⓓ break : repair _____

4. **Most likely, a *conundrum* is a type of**

   Ⓐ answer or explanation.   Ⓒ tailor or seamstress.

   Ⓑ riddle or puzzle.   Ⓓ crater or hole.

5. Look up the words *pedestrian* and *conundrum* in the dictionary. Write down what they mean.

   • pedestrian (*noun*): _____

   • pedestrian (*adjective*): _____

   • conundrum: _____

Next, rewrite the sentences on the back of this paper. Substitute <u>pedestrian</u> or <u>conundrum</u> for the underlined words.

   • The question "What came first: the chicken or the egg?" is a famous <u>riddle</u>.

   • Benjamin Franklin was not a <u>dull</u> man; after all, he invented swim fins so he could swim faster!

Finally, use the words *pedestrian* and *conundrum* in two sentences of your own.

Use What You Know 2

Directions: Go through the answer choices. Write down how the words you know are connected. Cross out the ones that do not have the same connection as the words in the question. The correct answer will be the one that is not crossed out.

Connection

1. **make : create** _____
   (A) ring : finger _____
   (B) necklace : neck _____
   (C) bracelet : wrist _____
   (D) increase : wax _____

2. **Most likely, if something *waxes* or is *waxing*, it is**
   (A) getting smaller.   (C) getting bigger.
   (B) staying the same size.   (D) staying awake.

Connection

3. **multiply : divide** _____
   (A) wane : increase _____
   (B) smile : grin _____
   (C) jump : leap _____
   (D) giggle : laugh _____

4. **Most likely, if something *wanes* or is *waning*, it is**
   (A) getting smaller.   (C) getting bigger.
   (B) staying awake.   (D) staying the same size.

5. **miniature : small**
   (A) broke : rich
   (B) bright : pedestrian
   (C) intrepid : brave
   (D) shattered : whole

6. **cheerfulness : happiness**
   (A) shovel : dig
   (B) axe : chop
   (C) ruler : measure
   (D) trepidation : dread

7. **Most likely, someone *intrepid* is**
   (A) fearful.
   (B) courageous.
   (C) tiny.
   (D) enormous.

8. **Most likely, one who feels *trepidation* is**
   (A) afraid.
   (B) happy.
   (C) sleepy.
   (D) brave.

Challenge: The prefix "in" made the words *intrepid* and *trepidation* nearly opposite in meaning. Can one feel trepidation but still act intrepid? Explain your answer on the back of this page.

Use What You Know 3

Directions: Read all the answer choices. Think about how the words are connected. Write this information on the line to the right. **If the words in the answer choices are connected in the same way, they cannot be the answer!** This is because there is only one correct answer.

Connection

1. *unknown word : unknown word*

   Ⓐ waxing : increasing   synonyms

   Ⓑ waning : decreasing

   Ⓒ playing : working

   Ⓓ begging : pleading

   Answer choices _____, _____, and _____ must be wrong because they are all

   _____. The correct answer is _____.

Connection

2. *unknown word : unknown word*

   Ⓐ yolk : yoke

   Ⓑ bother : annoy

   Ⓒ scene : seen

   Ⓓ dough : doe

   Answer choices _____, _____, and _____ must be wrong because they are all

   _____. The correct answer is _____.

Connection

3. *unknown word : unknown word*

   Ⓐ chicken : coop

   Ⓑ sheep : pen

   Ⓒ horse : corral

   Ⓓ cow : mammal

   Answer choices _____, _____, and _____ must be wrong because they are all

   _____. The correct answer is _____.

4. Write down four pairs of answer choices. Make three of them have the same link. See if a classmate can tell you what the right answer is!

   Ⓐ _____ : _____   Ⓒ _____ : _____

   Ⓑ _____ : _____   Ⓓ _____ : _____

Use What You Know 4

Directions: Read all the answer choices. Think about how the words are connected. Write this information on the line to the right. **If the words in the answer choices are connected in the same way, they cannot be the answer!** This is because there is only one correct answer.

Connection

1. ***unknown word : unknown word***

   (A) son : daughter _____

   (B) chef : restaurant _____

   (C) emperor : empress _____

   (D) guy : gal _____

   Answer choices _____, _____, and _____ must be wrong because they are all

   _____. The correct answer is _____.

2. ***unknown : unknown***

   (A) watermelon : fruit

   (B) sofa : furniture

   (C) dishwasher : appliance

   (D) painting : watercolor

3. ***unknown : unknown***

   (A) yoke : oxen

   (B) rope : knot

   (C) reins : horse

   (D) leash : dog

4. **amble : walk**

   (A) rip : shred

   (B) float : sink

   (C) exit : enter

   (D) praise : insult

5. **somnambulate : sleepwalk**

   (A) melt : harden

   (B) help : hurt

   (C) practice : rehearse

   (D) talk : listen

6. In Latin, the word *ambulo* means walk. What do you think *somnus* means?

   _____

7. If one suffers from *insomnia*, what do you think one has trouble doing?

   _____

8. An ambulance got its name because in long ago battles, the wounded would lie on the fields. Two men with stretchers or a cart would walk across the battlefield to the injured. They would treat the wounded or carry them away. Do you think of people walking when you think of today's ambulances? Tell why or why not.

   _____

   _____

Analogies in Writing

Directions: Think of a bee. Then, think of a person. Write down two ways a person might be thought of like a bee.

1. _____

2. _____

An analogy is a likeness in some ways between things that are otherwise unlike. Writers often use analogies to help the readers make pictures in their heads.

Directions: For #3–6, choose the set of words that best completes this sentence:

If a writer compares a person to a bee, the writer may want the reader to make a picture in his/her head of a(n) . . .

3. Ⓐ person who cooperates

   Ⓑ person who does not cooperate

4. Ⓐ weak and defenseless person

   Ⓑ person who will fiercely defend him- or herself

5. Ⓐ *indolent* person (not liking work, lazy)

   Ⓑ *diligent* person (industrious, working carefully and steadily)

6. Ⓐ a person who produces a good, lasting product

   Ⓑ a person who has nothing to show for him- or herself

Challenge: Make an analogy where you compare yourself, a person from history, or a person from a book (real or make-believe) to an animate creature. (If something is animate, it is living.) Use the words *indolent* and *diligent* in your answer. Use complete sentences.

_____ : _____
         (person)   *(animate creature)*

_____ is/am a _____

because _____

_____

_____

_____

_____

Analogies in Writing 2

Remember that an **analogy** is a likeness in some ways between things that are otherwise unlike.

Directions: Complete the sentence and write more sentences to finish each analogy. Make sure you use lots of descriptive words to help the reader make a picture in his or her head.

1. Her face was like a storm cloud because _____

    _____

    _____

2. A student is like an empty container because _____

    _____

    _____

3. A city is like a man-made jungle because _____

    _____

    _____

4. The Sahara desert is like a separate planet because _____

    _____

    _____

5. Teaching someone to read is like giving them money because _____

    _____

    _____

6. Passengers on a bus are like a box of chocolates because _____

    _____

    _____

7. A computer is like a third hand because _____

    _____

    _____

8. A _____ is like a _____

    because _____

    _____

Share one of your analogies with the class.

Far Out Analogies

Directions: Think outside the box! Make up analogies that are so far out that they can only be described as ridiculous and silly. Have fun and be creative!

- **Example:** hat : tarantula :: sock : leech
- **Link:** You don't want to find a tarantula in your hat, just like you don't want a leech in your sock!
- **Example:** marshmallow : sun :: hot dog : volcano
- **Link:** One would not roast a marshmallow over the sun, just as one would not roast a hot dog over a volcano.

1. swim : pudding :: dance : _____

    • **Link:** _____

    _____

2. comet : palace :: satellite : _____

    • **Link:** _____

    _____

3. consume : car :: drink : _____

    • **Link:** _____

    _____

4. neighbor : dinosaur :: _____ : _____

    • **Link:** _____

    _____

5. friendly : shark :: _____ : _____

    • **Link:** _____

    _____

6. _____ : _____ as _____ : _____

    • **Link:** _____

    _____

7. _____ : _____ as _____ : _____

    • **Link:** _____

    _____

Read one of your analogies to your classmates. Could anyone figure out the link?

Analogies in Reading

Directions: Read the passage. Answer the questions below.

"Lieutenant Colonel William Rankin is analogous to a raindrop," Deven said.

"How can someone be compared to a raindrop? That doesn't make sense," Mina responded.

"It does when you hear what he did. Rankin had to eject from his plane into a thunderstorm. He was at 47,000 feet (14.3 km). He suffered from immediate frostbite because the air temperature was colder than 50 degrees below zero. The air pressure was so low that he suffered from decompression. His eyes, ears, nose, and mouth started to bleed.

"What made him like a raindrop was that ten minutes after he normally would have landed, he was still in the air! He was being bounced up and down in the clouds! He had to keep his mouth closed so he wouldn't drown! He was being hit by hailstones! He could hear and feel thunder. Lightning blazed all around him. One time, he appeared to rise above his own parachute! How long was Rankin riding the wind? He landed 40 minutes after he ejected."

---

1. **The analogy between Rankin and a raindrop works because**

    Ⓐ Rankin ejected from a plane into a storm cloud.

    Ⓑ Rankin bounced like a raindrop in a storm cloud.

2. **Rankin would not be analogous to a raindrop if**

    Ⓐ raindrops always fell straight to the ground.

    Ⓑ he had not suffered from immediate frostbite.

3. **From the story, one can tell that**

    Ⓐ there was no risk of Rankin freezing to death.

    Ⓑ clouds can contain both frozen and unfrozen water.

Challenge: Look in books or on the Internet to find out more about Lieutenant Colonel William Rankin.

Analogies in Reading 2

Directions: Read the passage. Answer the questions.

Clair said, "Lina, you're like a dog on a bone with those riddles. You have to stop thinking about them. You have to bury them deep in your mind and forget about them."

"I can't," answered Lina. "I can't bury them deep enough. Besides, no matter how many times I bury them, I keep digging them up. They keep coming back to gnaw at me. I keep thinking that if I chew on them long enough, I'll finally crack them. Now I think those conundrums are impossible. After all, how can a man ride into town on Friday and leave on Wednesday but only stay two days? And how can a girl be born in 1805 but only be 15 today? And what can be added to a 110-pound (50 kilogram) barrel of water that will make it lighter? And what is it that from the beginning of eternity to the end of time and space is in every place?"

All of a sudden, Lina let out a whoop. "I've got it!" she cried. "The man was on a horse named Friday. The girl was born in a hospital room with the number 1805. All that needs to be added to the barrel is a hole, and it is the letter 'e' that is in every place from the beginning of *eternity* to the end of *time* and *space*."

1. **Why did Clair make an analogy between Lina and a dog on a bone?**

   Ⓐ Lina was chewing on a bone while she thought about the riddles.

   Ⓑ Lina could not stop thinking about the riddles, just like a dog cannot stop chewing on a bone.

2. **Find and underline these words in the story: *bury, gnaw, chew, crack*. Tell why using these words helped the reader picture Lina's reaction to the riddles.**

   _____

   _____

   _____

3. **Write a paragraph where you tell about a time when you could be compared to "a dog on a bone." Use some of the words from question 2 in your answer.**

   _____

   _____

   _____

   _____

   _____

Analogies in Reading 3

Directions: Read the passage. Answer the questions.

After hours of preening themselves in front of the mirror, Veronica and Connie were ready. They entered the stage dressed in headdresses of soft plumes that floated around their heads like feathery crowns. They proudly strutted and danced in brightly colored capes of blues and greens. In step, they grabbed their capes by their edges and held them open, revealing bright gemstones that were fastened to their shirts. It was if they had opened their wings to reveal brilliant eyes that reflected back onto the audience.

After the performance, Veronica and Connie stood in front of their manager, waiting to be told how well they had done. Their manager told them that their performance was superb. He also made an analogy to a certain animal.

---

1. **Most likely, the manager made an analogy between what animal and Veronica and Connie's performance?**

   Ⓐ alligator   Ⓑ stork   Ⓒ tiger   Ⓓ peacock

2. **Give two examples from the story that justify your answer to question 1.**

   • _____

   • _____

3. **Rewrite the first paragraph about Veronica and Connie's act. This time, make it so the manager would have to choose a different animal to make an analogy with. You may choose any animal you like.**

_____

_____

_____

_____

_____

_____

_____

_____

_____

Connection Review

Directions: Look at the word pairs in the first column. Think about how they are connected. Match the word pairs in the first column with a phrase from the second column that tells how they are connected. The first one has been done for you.

Hints: Use each phrase only once. If you do not know an answer right away, skip it. Come back to it at the end.

Word Pairs	How They Are Connected
__K__ 1. nuts : bolts	**A.** antonym (opposite)
_____ 2. hesitate : pause	**B.** synonym (same meaning)
_____ 3. moose : moose	**C.** homophone (same sound)
_____ 4. help : help	**D.** multiple-meaning word
_____ 5. planet : Saturn	**E.** adjective
_____ 6. encourage : discourage	**F.** classifying (group to member)
_____ 7. calculator : multiplying	**G.** past to present
_____ 8. their : there	**H.** one to more (plural)
_____ 9. governor : governess	**I.** purpose
_____ 10. ball : rubber	**J.** where things go
_____ 11. bee : hive	**K.** things or words that go together
_____ 12. drew : draw	**L.** male to female

Challenge: Write two sentences. In each sentence, use the multiple-meaning word from above in a different way.

1. _____

_____

2. _____

_____

Connection Review 2

Directions: Look at the word pairs in the first column. Think about how they are connected. Match the word pairs in the first column with a phrase from the second column that tells how they are connected. The first one has been done for you.

Hints: Use each phrase only once. If you do not know an answer right away, skip it. Come back to it at the end.

Word Pairs	How Connected
_L_ *1.* **pharmacist : drugstore**	**A.** antonym (opposite)
_____ *2.* **ewe : sheep**	**B.** synonym (same meaning)
_____ *3.* **wrapping paper : present**	**C.** homophone (same sound)
_____ *4.* **tide : tied**	**D.** less than/more than
_____ *5.* **horn : rhinoceros**	**E.** family names
_____ *6.* **idle : loaf**	**F.** what people use
_____ *7.* **gold : element**	**G.** part name to animal
_____ *8.* **whirlwind : tornado**	**H.** multiple-meaning word
_____ *9.* **moving : stationary**	**I.** outside or on top
_____ *10.* **astronomer : telescope**	**J.** classifying (member to group)
_____ *11.* **cactus : spiny**	**K.** adjective
_____ *12.* **wish : wish**	**L.** where work

Challenge: Write two sentences. In each sentence, use the multiple-meaning word from above in a different way.

1. _____

_____

2. _____

Practice Being the Teacher

Directions: It is your turn to teach. Look at the word pair in the box. Show how to find the answer to the analogy.

$$\boxed{\textbf{magnify : enlarge}}$$

Ⓐ trap : release   Ⓒ copy : duplicate

Ⓑ pine : tree   Ⓓ collect : spread

1. First, write out how the words in the question are connected.

   • When you __m_____, you __e_____.

   Next, try out the connection with the other word pairs.

   Ⓐ When you __t_____, you __r_____.

   Ⓑ When you __p_____, you __t_____.

   Ⓒ When you __c_____, you __d_____.

   Ⓓ When you __c_____, you __s_____.

2. Answers _____ and _____ cannot be right because they have the same connection. They are both _____. (*synonyms* or *antonyms*)

3. Answer _____ cannot be right because the words in the word pair are not _____. (*synonyms* or *antonyms*)

---

4. What would the answer be if the question were $\boxed{\textbf{hold : held}}$?

   Ⓐ ground : grind   Ⓒ judge : courtroom

   Ⓑ went : go   Ⓓ broadcast : broadcast

5. Answers _____ and _____ are wrong because the verb tense is written in the wrong order. It should be _____ *to* _____, not _____ *to* _____.

6. Answer _____ is wrong because the words are not connected in the same way. The word __j_____ is not the past tense of _____.

Practice Being the Teacher 2

Directions: It is your turn to teach. Look at the word pair in the box. Show how to find the answer to the analogy.

map : navigate

(A) overcome : conquer   (C) entertain : amuse

(B) weigh : scale   (D) kiln : bake

1. First, write out how the words in the question are connected.

   • You use a <u>m   </u> to <u>n   </u> .

   Next, try out the connection with the other word pairs.

   (A) You use a <u>o   </u> to <u>c   </u> .

   (B) You use a <u>w   </u> to <u>s   </u> .

   (C) You use an <u>e   </u> to <u>a   </u> .

   (D) You use a <u>k   </u> to <u>b   </u> .

2. Answers _____ and _____ cannot be right because they have the same connection.
   They are both _____. (*synonyms* or *antonyms*)

3. Answer _____ cannot be right because it is in the wrong order.

---

4. What would the answer be if the question was **Tyrannosaurus Rex : dinosaur** ?

   (A) reptile : boa constrictor   (C) kangaroo : mammal

   (B) poison dart frogs : amphibian (D) spider : tarantula

5. Answer _____ is wrong because the first item is plural (more than one).

6. Answers _____ and _____ are wrong because they are written in the wrong order.

---

7. Write an analogy with four answer choices. Only one answer choice should be correct.
   Teach the class how to solve it.

   _____ : _____

   (A) _____ : _____   (C) _____ : _____

   (B) _____ : _____   (D) _____ : _____

Practice What You Know

Directions: Find the answer that best completes each analogy. Remember to . . .

- pay attention to word order
- think about how the words are connected
- read every answer choice
- cross out the ones that can't be right.

---

1. lass : lad
- Ⓐ knight : lady
- Ⓑ czar : czarina
- Ⓒ host : hostess
- Ⓓ princess : prince

2. refund : repay
- Ⓐ rebel : revolt
- Ⓑ refuel : rest
- Ⓒ regret : rely
- Ⓓ resent : reset

3. card : deck
- Ⓐ mosaic : tile
- Ⓑ cell : bar
- Ⓒ piece : puzzle
- Ⓓ cup : teaspoon

4. splinter : wood
- Ⓐ castle : hut
- Ⓑ shard : glass
- Ⓒ school : classroom
- Ⓓ dormitory : bed

5. jelly : jar
- Ⓐ groceries : bag
- Ⓑ basin : water
- Ⓒ phone : talk
- Ⓓ shell : peanut

6. school : fish
- Ⓐ cattle : herd
- Ⓑ flock : sheep
- Ⓒ puppy : litter
- Ⓓ ink : squid

7. led : lead
- Ⓐ started : ended
- Ⓑ ended : started
- Ⓒ began : begin
- Ⓓ begin : began

8. got : get
- Ⓐ think : thought
- Ⓑ pet : petted
- Ⓒ feel : felt
- Ⓓ hopped : hop

9. common : rare
- Ⓐ crook : thief
- Ⓑ cuddle : snuggle
- Ⓒ curse : swear
- Ⓓ cruel : kind

10. plateau : flat
- Ⓐ wet : swamp
- Ⓑ desert : arid
- Ⓒ jagged : peak
- Ⓓ sandy : beach

11. cat : cougar
- Ⓐ dog : bark
- Ⓑ sedan : car
- Ⓒ bird : swallow
- Ⓓ pick : tool

12. minute : second
- Ⓐ week : day
- Ⓑ calendar : time
- Ⓒ month : year
- Ⓓ decade : century

Challenge: Make an analogy with the name of a musician (living or dead) or a band and his/her/its type of music or instrument they play. Use other musicians and types of music for answer choices. Only one answer should be correct.

_____ : _____

     (musician or band)   (type of music or instrument)

Ⓐ _____ : _____   Ⓒ _____ : _____

Ⓑ _____ : _____   Ⓓ _____ : _____

Be prepared to tell which of your answers is correct and why.

Practice What You Know 2

Directions: Find the answer that best completes each analogy. Remember to . . .

- pay attention to word order
- read every answer choice
- think about how the words are connected
- cross out the ones that can't be right.

1. **limb : person**
   - Ⓐ twig : bush
   - Ⓑ leopard : spot
   - Ⓒ fur : sea lion
   - Ⓓ foot : hand

2. **species : species**
   - Ⓐ kinds : kind
   - Ⓑ type : types
   - Ⓒ varieties : variety
   - Ⓓ sorts : sort

3. **siren : warn**
   - Ⓐ nail : hammer
   - Ⓑ play : piano
   - Ⓒ listen : radio
   - Ⓓ pager : alert

4. **mouse : scampers**
   - Ⓐ slithers : eel
   - Ⓑ flutters : moth
   - Ⓒ duck : waddles
   - Ⓓ scurries : rat

5. **cellar : house**
   - Ⓐ attic : roof
   - Ⓑ dungeon : castle
   - Ⓒ barn : loft
   - Ⓓ canyon : ravine

6. **strict : rigid**
   - Ⓐ harsh : tender
   - Ⓑ nervous : unruffled
   - Ⓒ scrawl : scribble
   - Ⓓ firm : unstable

7. **mitt : catch**
   - Ⓐ racquet : ball
   - Ⓑ play : field
   - Ⓒ slide : base
   - Ⓓ bat : hit

8. **islet : island**
   - Ⓐ town : city
   - Ⓑ ocean : puddle
   - Ⓒ mountain : hill
   - Ⓓ giant : dwarf

9. **talon : claw**
   - Ⓐ fur : hair
   - Ⓑ ear : hear
   - Ⓒ leg : tail
   - Ⓓ hoof : neck

10. **wheel : cart**
    - Ⓐ guitar : strum
    - Ⓑ spoon : sip
    - Ⓒ pedal : bicycle
    - Ⓓ broom : sweep

11. **merchant : sells**
    - Ⓐ paints : artist
    - Ⓑ acts : actor
    - Ⓒ astronaut : space
    - Ⓓ farmer : cultivates

12. **enchant : disgust**
    - Ⓐ merge : unite
    - Ⓑ wax : wane
    - Ⓒ custom : habit
    - Ⓓ mingle : blend

Challenge: Make answer choices for this word pair: | **dandelion : weed** |. Make sure only one answer choice is correct.

Ⓐ _____ : _____   Ⓒ _____ : _____

Ⓑ _____ : _____   Ⓓ _____ : _____

Which answer is correct? _____ Why? _____

_____

_____

Answer Sheets

These sheets may be used to provide practice in answering questions in a standardized-test format.

Student's Name: _____

_____

Activity Page: _____

1. Ⓐ   Ⓑ   Ⓒ   Ⓓ
2. Ⓐ   Ⓑ   Ⓒ   Ⓓ
3. Ⓐ   Ⓑ   Ⓒ   Ⓓ
4. Ⓐ   Ⓑ   Ⓒ   Ⓓ
5. Ⓐ   Ⓑ   Ⓒ   Ⓓ
6. Ⓐ   Ⓑ   Ⓒ   Ⓓ
7. Ⓐ   Ⓑ   Ⓒ   Ⓓ
8. Ⓐ   Ⓑ   Ⓒ   Ⓓ
9. Ⓐ   Ⓑ   Ⓒ   Ⓓ
10. Ⓐ   Ⓑ   Ⓒ   Ⓓ
11. Ⓐ   Ⓑ   Ⓒ   Ⓓ
12. Ⓐ   Ⓑ   Ⓒ   Ⓓ

Student's Name: _____

_____

Activity Page: _____

1. Ⓐ   Ⓑ   Ⓒ   Ⓓ
2. Ⓐ   Ⓑ   Ⓒ   Ⓓ
3. Ⓐ   Ⓑ   Ⓒ   Ⓓ
4. Ⓐ   Ⓑ   Ⓒ   Ⓓ
5. Ⓐ   Ⓑ   Ⓒ   Ⓓ
6. Ⓐ   Ⓑ   Ⓒ   Ⓓ
7. Ⓐ   Ⓑ   Ⓒ   Ⓓ
8. Ⓐ   Ⓑ   Ⓒ   Ⓓ
9. Ⓐ   Ⓑ   Ⓒ   Ⓓ
10. Ⓐ   Ⓑ   Ⓒ   Ⓓ
11. Ⓐ   Ⓑ   Ⓒ   Ⓓ
12. Ⓐ   Ⓑ   Ⓒ   Ⓓ

Answer Key

Introducing Analogies (page 4)
1. kitten
2. quack
3. herd
4. feather
5. any bird type
7. mother
8. brother
9. aunt
10. nephew
11. daughter
12. uncle or father

Synonyms in Analogies (page 5)
1. A 5. C
2. D 6. B
3. B 7. C
4. A 8. D

Antonyms in Analogies (page 6)
1. B 5. A
2. C 6. D
3. D 7. A
4. B 8. C

Synonym and Antonym Practice (page 7)
1. A, synonyms
2. B, antonyms
3. C, antonyms
4. D, synonyms
5. B, antonyms
6. B, synonyms
7. C, synonyms
8. A, antonyms
9. A, synonyms
10. D, synonyms
11. C, antonyms
12. B, synonyms

Plurals (page 9)
1. A 7. D
2. B 8. A
3. C 9. B
4. B 10. C
5. A 11. D
6. D

Adjectives (page 10)
1. feather; adjective
2. down; adjective
3. D
4. B
5. D

6. B
7. C
8. A
9. D
10. C
11. A

What People Use (page 11)
1. A 6. C
2. C 7. D
3. B 8. B
4. D 9. D
5. A

Things that Go Together (page 12)
1. B 5. A
2. D 6. A
3. C 7. D
4. C 8. B

Past and Present (page 13)
1. found
2. wept
3. sell
4. forget
5. made
6. fling
7. take
8. hurt
9. withstood
10. spread
11. present to past: 1, 2, 5, 9;
  past to present: 3, 4, 6, 7;
  can't tell: 8, 10; synonym:
  1, 2, 5, 6; antonym: 3, 4, 7, 9

Past and Present 2 (page 14)
1. A
2. B
3. D
4. C
5. B
6. B
7. C
8. A
9. D
10. C
11. Answers will vary (e.g., *fix,*
  cure, mend, repair).
12. unwind
13. Answer should rhyme with
  wound (e.g., *sound, pound*)

Purpose (page 15)
1. A
2. B
3. D
4. C
5. A
6. A
7. D
8. B
9. D
10. C
11–12. barometer : air pressure;
  anemometer : wind speed;
  hygrometer : humidity

Where Things Go (page 16)
1. B 6. C
2. A 7. D
3. B 8. B
4. C 9. A
5. A 10. D

Animal Family Names (page 17)
1. A 6. D
2. B 7. A
3. D 8. C
4. D 9. C
5. B 10. A

Finding the Connection (page 18)
1. D
2. A
3. B
4. what covers, or inside to
  outside
6. C
7. A
8. D
9. what goes in something
11. B
12. C
13. D
14. what flows through

Answer Key *(cont.)*

Finding the Connection 2 (page 19)
1. D
2. B
3. C
4. similar animal parts
6. D
7. B
8. A
9. part to animal, not animal to part
11. C
12. C
13. A
14. female to male

Finding the Connection 3 (page 20)
1. B
2. C
3. D
4. person and place where he/she works
6. A
7. C
8. B
9. movement/sound of animals
11. A
12. D
13. A
14. things that stick on, together, or in

Trying out the Connection (page 21)
1. swing, playground
2. mingle, blend
3. period, punctuation
4. D
5. C
6. A

Part to Whole (page 22)
1. A
2. C
3. D
4. B
5. A
6. B
7. B
8. C
9. D

10. D
11. A
12. C
13. part to whole: 1, 3, 4, 6, 9, 12; whole to part: 2, 5, 7, 8, 10, 11
14. (order may vary) pitcher : baseball team :: forward : soccer team

Less Than/More Than (page 23)
1. B
2. A
3. C
4. A
5. B
6. A
7. B
8. D
9. C
10. D
11. C

Classifying Analogies (page 24)
1. vegetables
2. furniture
3. A table is always a piece of furniture; A piece of furniture is not always a table.
4. C
5. B
6. A
7. D
8. B
9. C
10. A
11. D
12. B
Challenge: Australia; any other country

Classifying Analogies 2 (page 25)
1. dogs
2. A poodle is always a dog; A dog is not always a poodle.
3. B
4. C
5. A
6. D
7. D
8. C
9. B
10. A
11. B

Multiple-Meaning Words (page 27)
1. B
2. B
3. A
4. A
5. B
6. A
7. A
8. B
9. B
10. A

Multiple-Meaning Words 2 (page 28)
1. C
2. A, antonyms
3. D, synonyms
4. B, synonyms
5. D, synonyms
6. C, antonyms
7. A, synonyms
8. B, synonyms
9. A, synonyms
10. B, synonyms
11. D, you string beads
12. C, string is a thin rope
13. portion; to divide and give out

Math (page 29)
1. D
2. A
3. D
4. B
5. B
6. C
7. A
8. C

Math 2 (page 30)
1. C
2. D
3. C
4. A
5. A
6. B
7. D
8. B
9. D
10. C
11. ocean : glass
12. tree : forest

Answer Key *(cont.)*

Social Studies (page 31)
1. Australia
2. Canada
3. Mexico
4. France
5. Afghanistan
6. United Kingdom
7. Japan
8. Argentina
9. India
10. Singapore
11. Denmark
12. Egypt

Challenge: South Africa has 3 capitals (Pretoria : executive; Bloemfontein : judicial; Cape Town : legislative); Bolivia has two capitals (La Paz : administrative; Sucre : constitutional).

Social Studies 2 (page 32)
1. Africa
2. South America
3. Asia
4. North America
5. Asia
6. Africa
7. Asia
8. South America
9. Australia
10. Europe
11. Asia
12. North America

Challenge: Antarctica; too cold for running water

Science (page 33)
1. C
2. A
3. B
4. B
5. D
6. A
7. D
8. C
9. B
10. D

Science 2 (page 34)
1. primary consumer
2. secondary consumer
3. decomposer
4. producer
5. primary consumer
6. tertiary consumer
7. decomposer
8. producer
9. secondary consumer
10. tertiary consumer

Challenge: primary = fruits, vegetables, etc; secondary = food from herbivores (hamburger, turkey, etc.); tertiary = food from carnivore (shark fin soup, etc.)

Skeleton Analogies (page 35)
1. femur
2. metatarsus
3. tibia
4. tarsus
5. tail
6. sternum
7. phalanges
8. mandible

Challenge: same bone number (around 320), though bone shape and size depends on breed

Spelling (page 36)
1. a lot
2. all together
3. already
4. allot
5. altogether
6. all ready
7. a lot
8. allot
9. all ready
10. altogether
11. all together
12. already

Challenge: all together; Altogether

Homophones (page 37)
1-3. (any order) They sound alike, they have different spellings, and they are not synonyms.
1. sight
2. peer
3. stationary
4. site
5. their
6. they're
7. stationery
8. pier
9. there
10. cite

Homophones 2 (page 38)
They sound alike, they have different spellings, and they are not synonyms. (*Weight* means "how much something weighs"; *wait* means "to remain or stay.")
1. idle
2. its
3. weather
4. idol
5. aloud
6. whether
7. it's
8. allowed
9. I scream for ice cream.
10. Let us eat lettuce.

All Things Time (page 39)
1. C
2. A
3. D
4. B
5. B
6. C
7. D
8. C
9. B
10. A

Fearful Analogies (page 40)
1. D
2. C
3. B
4. A
5. D
6. A
7. B
8. C
9. insects; fish
10. "beautiful writing"

Inventions of the Century (page 41)
1. D
2. A
3. C
4. A
5. B
6. C
7. D
8. B
9. D
10. A

Answer Key *(cont.)*

Review of Analogy Types (page 42)
1. D, adjective
2. B, antonym
3. A, past/present
4. C, synonym
5. B, what people use
6. D, plural
7. C, synonym
8. C, adjective
9. A, what people use
10. B, plural
11. D, antonym
12. A, past/present
13. One can't know at first what the connection is.

Review of Analogy Types 2 (page 43)
1. A, member to group
2. C, less/more
3. B, homophone
4. D, where found
5. C, purpose
6. A, homophone
7. D, male/female
8. D, male/female
9. B, where found
10. C, less/more
11. A, member to group
12. B, purpose
13. all "yes"

Use What You Know (page 44)
1. A (member to group), B (synonyms), and D (way it's used) are not antonyms, so C is correct.
2. D
3. The question words are synonyms. B (antonyms), C (use), and D (antonyms) are not synonyms, so the answer must be A.
4. B

Use What You Know 2 (page 45)
1. The question words are synonyms. A, B, and C are where you wear things, so the answer must be D.
2. C
3. The question words are opposites. B, C, and D are synonyms (or less to more), so the answer must be A.
4. A
5. C
6. D
7. B
8. A

Use What You Know 3 (page 46)
1. A, B, D are all synonyms, so C (antonym) is correct.
2. A, C, D are all homophones, so B (synonym) is correct.
3. A, B, C are all about things and where they are kept, so D (member to group) is correct.

Use What You Know 4 (page 47)
1. A, C, D are all male to female, so B (where person works) is correct.
2. D
3. B
4. A
5. C
6. sleep
7. sleeping

Analogies in Writing (page 48)
3. A
4. B
5. B
6. A

Analogies in Reading (page 51)
1. B
2. A
3. B

Analogies in Reading (page 52)
1. B

Analogies in Reading 3 (page 53)
1. D
2. strutted, feathery crowns, opened wings, brilliant eyes

Connection Review (page 54)
1. K
2. B
3. H
4. D
5. F
6. A
7. I
8. C
9. L
10. E
11. J
12. G

Connection Review 2 (page 55)
1. L
2. E
3. I
4. C
5. G
6. B
7. J
8. D
9. A
10. F
11. K
12. H

Practice Being the Teacher (page 56)
2. A and D; antonyms
3. B; synonyms
4. D
5. A and B; present to past, not past to present
6. C; judge, courtroom

Practice Being the Teacher 2 (page 57)
2. A and C, synonyms
3. B
4. C
5. B
6. A and D

Practice What You Know (page 58)
1. D
2. A
3. C
4. B
5. A
6. B
7. C
8. D
9. D
10. B
11. C
12. A

Practice What You Know 2 (page 59)
1. A
2. B
3. D
4. C
5. B
6. C
7. D
8. A
9. A
10. C
11. D
12. B